The traveling gourmet

VENICE

AND ITS REGIONS

Acknowledgements:
Liana Levi and
Alexandre Melissinos

The editor's special thanks to
Michel, Nathalie, and Grana of *L'Osteria*.

Thanks also to
craftsman Alberto Valese
of Santo Stefano,
who supplied the design
for the endpapers.

Design:
Marine Gille
Translation:
Louise Guiney
Copy-editing and typesetting:
Corinne Orde
Photoengraving:
Sele Offset Torino, Srl, Italy
Printing:
JCG, Barcelona, Spain
© Photos Mark Edward Smith
© Photos Bruno Morandi/Hoaqui
for pages 30 (top right), 55, 107
(top center), 122 (right),
138 (left), 139 (top left)

Originally published as
L'Esprit du Goût: de Venise à Vérone
© 1999 Plume
English-language edition
© 2001 Flammarion

ISBN 2-08010-552-3
FA0552-01-V
Dépôt légal: 05/2001

The traveling gourmet
VENICE
AND ITS REGIONS

Text by Gilles Plazy
Photographs by Mark E. Smith
Recipes by Toni Vianello

Flammarion

CONTENTS

INTRODUCTION

In the northeast corner of Italy between the sea and the mountains—the Adriatic and the Alps—lies the *Regione Veneto*, also bordered by Lake Garda and the Po valley, with Venice the jewel in its crown. Originally a distant colonial outpost of Latinate Rome, Venice has always turned its face toward the Germanic north and Byzantine east (the other side of the mountain; the other side of the sea), an Italian city that keeps its own counsel and is perfectly at ease with the concept of "Europe." It has long been open to the rest of the world. Its renowned ambassador Marco Polo blazed a trail between Venice and China at a time when the world of the Mandarins was totally unknown to the West. Rooted in an amazingly stable republican regime, the power of Venice was maritime, commercial, and diplomatic. Even before gaining ascendance over its own region, it had already spread its tentacles to the eastern shores of the Mediterranean. The lion of Saint Mark eventually roamed inland, however, staying until the bas-reliefs symbolizing Venetian supremacy were

THE ANGEL ATOP SAINT MARK'S BELL-TOWER GAZING OUT OVER THE LAGOON.

removed by Napoleon Bonaparte from every wall on which they appeared. The power of the doges, a rank instituted in the seventh century, was eroded by the revolutionary fervor that inflamed all of Europe at the dawn of the modern era, and which here favored the supremacy of Austria. It was not until Venice joined the Kingdom of Italy that peace was finally restored.

Today the city occupies a unique position. Because of its geographical site and the fact it is built on a lagoon; because of its history, the vestiges of which have been particularly well preserved (there are still 334 palaces in the city); its artistic heritage; and the serene image it has managed to retain, Venice is undoubtedly the most fascinating city in the world. Although the Veneto region as a whole has of course reaped benefits from this fame, it has suffered as well. Too many people fail to realize that behind the gorgeous mask of the city whose name it bears lie other wonderful cities, landscapes,

THE MAGNIFICENCE OF THE DOGES IS NO MORE, BUT THIS WOMAN PEEKING AROUND THE SHUTTER ENJOYS A QUALITY OF LIFE THAT STILL SURVIVES.

Padua, Vicenza, Treviso, the valleys of the Adige and the Po, Lake Garda. An entire region offers the wealth of a diverse topography and innumerable important monuments and works of art. The Veneto has a distinctive character, combining aloof independence with a love of the exotic, an entrepreneurial spirit with a taste for pleasure. The region's internecine rivalries were extinguished by Venice's policy of wooing rather than subduing, and forming alliances with artistic Padua and fortified Verona. Conscious of its own unique status, Venice has never tried to force others into the same mold. Today Venice thus stands slightly apart from the Veneto, a region of Italy more delicately balanced than any other between the dual claims of the eternal and the temporal. You sit at a café on the Zattere. You order a glass of *Soave* or *Valpolicella*. As you watch, a large boat glides by—a modern monster of water-borne tourism. And yet, it's as lovely as a dream by Federico Fellini. Tomorrow you'll go to the Lido or Verona, to Lake Garda or the Dolomites. You are off on a voyage of discovery into the purest bliss.

VENICE AND THE SEA

Venice is a city of the impossible: conceived with incredible daring and built on shifting sands in a lagoon that until the end of the nineteenth century was cut off from the mainland—referred to locally as *Terra Firma*. That mad daring sealed the fate of this Venus, risen from the waves to reign over the Mediterranean as an astute commercial and maritime power, virtually the center of the world. The center, that is, until the Portuguese had the devastating idea of sailing around the Cape of Good Hope, thus opening sea routes to the treasures at the ends of the earth that Marco Polo had been able to reach only by land. Today, Venice defies time and gravity, continuing to project an astounding beauty undiminished by age: a miracle of architecture, combining the Medieval, Renaissance, and Baroque eras; a stupefying series of palaces lining the broad canal in which their foundations rest; an improbable place that can only be visited by boat or on foot, from bridge to bridge, a journey through a labyrinth in which history has been trapped; a museum-city rivaling Rome and Florence for first place as a gem of the Renaissance—that pivotal point in world history experienced by the city through some of the period's greatest artists, or at least the warmest and liveliest.

An emblematic scene: the doge, accompanied by dignitaries of the Most Serene Venetian Republic and foreign ambassadors, steps into the sumptuous official barge known as the *Bucintoro*. It has no sails and is propelled into the open sea off the Lido by oarsmen whose rhythmic strokes cut neatly into the lagoon. Imagine an occasion, Ascension Day, *La Sensa*. All of Christendom is celebrating the glory of Christ risen after his bodily death. Venice, as queen of the Mediterranean, adds her own special pageantry to the ritual. The doge casts a golden ring into the sea, proclaiming: "We wed you, O Sea, as

a sign of true and perpetual dominion." Venice has indeed won dominion over the sea. Her survival depends on a marriage with the water surrounding her. For eight centuries, despite the city's declining power, the ritual was celebrated every year, until the day when Napoleon Bonaparte, who could not tolerate glories competing with his own, and whose troops had crossed Italy in triumph, put an end to the ceremony and converted the *Bucintoro* into a prison. Tangible proof, reflecting the soul of a city that has never abandoned its maritime vocation, is nevertheless still visible at the Correr Museum, in the form of numerous paintings and scale models. The more modest gondola, still a common sight and a ubiquitous tourist cliché, is also emblematic of Venice. The gondola is narrow vessel rising at each end to a crescent-shaped point high above the water. Its curved construction makes it possible for the gondolier to propel it with a single pole attached to the stern, where he stands to manipulate the pole on either side of the vessel. A more traditional, straight-hulled boat would turn in circles if propelled in this way, but the gondola's shape corrects the natural thrust and moves the boat forward.

NARROW CANALS OFTEN
PROVIDE JUST ENOUGH
OPEN SPACE FOR A
SHAFT OF SUNLIGHT TO
FALL ON THE CROWDED
ROWS OF HOUSE LINING
THEM.

THE FEE-SYSTEM FOR
GONDOLIERS—WHO
HAVE OFTEN PLIED
THEIR TRADE FROM
FATHER TO SON FOR
GENERATIONS—IS
STRICTLY CONTROLLED
(ABOVE).

GONDOLAS ARE CURVED
SO THEY CAN BE
STEERED USING A
SINGLE POLE. THESE
EXTREMELY ELABORATE
MODELS ARE USED
PRIMARILY FOR
TOURISTS. A GONDOLA
RIDE AROUND THE
CENTER OF VENICE
COSTS ABOUT
200,000 LIRE.

This unique type of boat was first desi-gned in the eleventh century (if not before), and until the nineteenth century served for all transportation along the canals of Venice. The gondola has now largely been replaced by the motor-boat—municipal *vaporetti* and privately owned craft—here used as other cities use the car, which has no place in Venice. This allows the streets and squares (*campi*) to be used for lei-surely strolling and to resonate with the sound of voices bet-ween their walls.

Venice possesses the haunting beauty of a mirage. Even when we've seen it a thousand times in pictures, we may still suspect it of being a misleading lure or an illusion. We are thus eager to wit-ness for ourselves the city everyone should see at least once in a lifetime, or so it is said; the city consi-dered to be the tourist holy-of-holies. But Venice will not bare its soul to harried tourists any more than the Mona Lisa will reveal her secret during a thirty-second museum stampede. Those who take a quick tour of Saint Mark's, hop into a gon-dola, sample a risotto, and snap a few photos will actually have seen nothing. Venice, at first sight so imposing,

THE CAMPO SAN ZAN DEGOLA IN THE SANTA CROCE SECTION.

ACQUA ALTA: SEVERAL TIMES EACH WINTER, THE WATERS OF THE LAGOON FLOOD SAINT MARK'S SQUARE. PEDESTRIANS KEEP THEIR FEET DRY BY WALKING INDIAN-FILE OVER TEMPORARY WOODEN FOOTBRIDGES.

spectacular, and grandiose—whether rising from the lagoon before the marveling eyes of those arriving from the sea, or sweeping those emerging from the railroad station into the bustle along the Grand Canal—has too many riches, secrets, memories, and hidden passageways for facile conquest. The Venice that has successfully resisted aggression also resists love, and those seeking to possess her (some pretend they have found the key) are merely pretentious lovers lured into believing that a few shared favors are the same as total submission. They will never pierce that abiding mystery, the heart and soul of Venice. It will thus come as no surprise to learn that so many imaginations have

been inflamed over the centuries by this city that has served as a backdrop for great love stories, a subject continuously revisited by the greatest or most ordinary of painters, an inspiration or stumbling-block for writers stimulated by its mystery.

Every year eight million tourists come to admire, in more or less haste and more or less superficially, this treasure of the world's artistic heritage. They come for its beauty, for its unique charm and consummate skill in seeming to have eluded the march of time, and also for the way in which it seems to float atop the waves. The stones of its palaces have been eroded by the dirty waters churned up by motor-boats. Their façades have also been

A CITY MADE FOR LOVERS.

THE CHURCH OF SAN GIORGIO MAGGIORE FACES THE DOGES' PALACE AND THE "PIAZZETTA". IN THE FOREGROUND, A COLUMN BEARING THE EMBLEM OF VENICE, THE LION.

damaged by an atmosphere filled with the industrial pollution emitted by the numerous factories close by. And there is not as much money as there once was for maintaining dilapidated palaces. The problem is urgent: Venice must be saved. It must be protected against the inexorable rise of the water around it, against the throngs of people suffocating it, and against itself, with its tendency—in a spirit of melancholy detachment—to let things ride.

Forecasts for the future are chilling: subsidence of the city into the water surrounding it and the sand beneath it; the disintegration of palaces standing on eroded foundations; a return to the void Saint Mark saw when he first landed on a deserted island and heard the voice prophesying that one day his mortal remains would rest there, honored by the people of a great city. Thus has legend added color to Venice's prehistory. On the other hand, it is true that the remains of the evangelist were stolen from Alexandria, and that a basilica was built in Venice to contain them. Of the four chroniclers who recounted the life of Christ, Mark is the one represented by a lion, the royal beast proud Venice had no compunction in adopting as its own emblem; but with a difference: the Venetian lion is usually depicted with its front paws on land and its hindquarters in the water— a reminder of the city's uniquely precarious situation.

THE CRYPT OF THE BASILICA OF SAINT MARK'S.

SAINT MARK'S BELL-TOWER.

VENICE IS OFTEN
VEILED IN MIST. THE
CHURCH OF THE
REDEEMER ON THE ISLE
OF LA GIUDECCA.

GIOVANNI
GREVEMBROCH, *TWO
VENETIANS WEARING
THE BAUTA.*
WATERCOLOR IN THE
CORRER MUSEUM

When rising tides are accompanied by high winds, the water can no longer be held at bay. It pours into the city's streets and floods the Piazza San Marco (Saint Mark's Square). Pedestrian access to the main arteries is provided by temporary footbridges built on wooden trestles, and boots become a practical necessity rather than a fashion statement. This is *Acqua Alta*, as the resigned Venetians refer to it. The Nobel prize-winning poet Joseph Brodsky, now buried in San Michele cemetery, wrote a long poem on the phenomenon. One proposed solution would involve closing off the three remaining entrances to the port, on either side of the Lido, with floodgates when necessary, and many other more or less viable suggestions have been made. But the preservation of an ecological heritage as complex as this one presents a problem comparable to squaring the circle or determining the sex of angels. Angels and sexuality have their relevance to Venice, by the way: the angel that guarded the city from atop San Giorgio Maggiore was struck by lightning some years ago; and the Venice carnival features disguise and cross-dressing, the appeal of which depends on expressing one's sexual orientation (whatever it might be) without constraint. But Venice herself is clearly feminine, her name and very existence recalling that of a goddess risen

SAILBOATS MOORED IN
THE PORT OF SAN
GIORGIO MAGGIORE.

from the waves too explicitly for there to
be any doubt. A spectacular event used
to be held at mid-carnival time: the Flight
of the Angel. An acrobat would ascend the
bell-tower, perform daring feats there,
and then, by means of a double rope,
would abseil down to the ground, landing
at the feet of the doge—an appropriate
symbol for a city with a genius for diplo-
macy (or falling on one's feet!). Then
there came a day—although not
the one set aside for the Flight
of the Angel and, in fact, long
after that tradition had disap-
peared—when the bell-tower
itself fell to the ground (an
event captured on film). The
Venetians rebuilt their tower —
from which Goethe had first
seen the sea (the Adriatic, on the far side
of the Lido)—just as it had been before,
and on top of its spire they placed a gilded angel, there to revolve continuously
in the wind.

Perdition—an ineluctable fate according to the doomsayers—perhaps explains
the melancholy some believe to be the very
essence of Venice. Thomas Mann, in a
work (*Death in Venice*) written early in
the twentieth century and later filmed by
Luchino Visconti with Dirk Bogarde, further exploited a type of Venetian melancholy—the relatively modern affliction of
consumptive *morbidezza*—already being
mined at the height of the romantic
period (Alfred de Musset, betrayed by

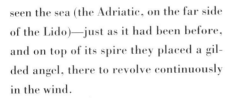

LOBBY OF THE
EXCELSIOR HOTEL

THE GRAND CANAL
NEAR THE RIALTO
BRIDGE.

George Sand, lying ill in his room at the
Danieli where a kind physician attends
him ...), and since then several dandies
are known to have taken their own lives
in the city. It is true that the stench of
putrefaction wafting from the canals and
the fog so often veiling the lagoon can give
the city and its inhabitants a ghostly cast
which, when combined with nostalgia for
a glorious past, might easily
arouse the pernicious reveries
of self-styled Pierrots. But
then carnival ringleader
Harlequin steps in, offering an antidote made from
equal doses of pleasure
and charming insolence.
And Casanova, who during

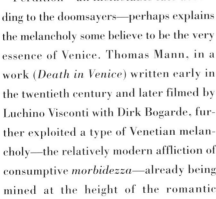

THE ONLY PORTRAIT OF
CASANOVA PAINTED
FROM LIFE.
GIACOMO CASANOVA WAS
BORN IN VENICE ON
APRIL 2ND, 1725, ON
THE CALLE MALIPIERO
NEAR THE CAMPO SAN
SAMUELE.

on wooden piles sunk deep into the loose sand at the bottom of the water. Unlike other great cities envied by their rivals, Venice has never been sacked by its enemies. It has always been shown as much respect by those occupying it as by those native to it. This explains why it has remained virtually unchanged over the centuries, sustaining its own distinctive imprint but not misled by illusory youth. Venice, old but sublime, is determined to be eternal. The lagoon, a victim of over-modernization (its delicate equilibrium destroyed by the Marghera port complex) and its own success (too many visitors use it and abuse it), may still hold unpleasant surprises in store. However, in the face of dire prophecies, the people of Venice have set to work, diligently restoring the damage and devising imaginative solutions to their problems. In this endeavor, they can count on help from people all over the world, because Venice, more than any other city, has given them the sense that it also belongs to them.

THE ENTRANCE TO THE
PALAZZO BARBARO ON
THE GRAND CANAL.

the unfettered eighteenth century embodied what we might call, quoting Milan Kundera, "the unbearable lightness of being," remains the eternal symbol of Venetian pleasure-seeking. Venice, more than any other city, has remained true to itself: a daughter of Byzantium that denied obeisance to Rome (the doges were not unduly impressed by the pope), to Paris (submitting only briefly to Napoleon's imperial will), and to Vienna (the city's proud beauty was also conquered by the emperor of Austria). Constantly exercising her right to the title "Most Serene," Venice survived, supporting her stones

One should visit Venice with an open mind and no preconceived ideas, ready for an experience intensified by its brevity. Ideally, one should never have read or seen anything to do with Venice—but of course this is impossible. At least one can try, not to possess Venice, but to be possessed by her, to accept the mirror she holds out. That mirror will reveal you to yourself: harried tourist, casual stroller, cultivated historian, obsessive art lover,

THE BRIDGE OF SIGHS
ONCE LINKED THE
CITY'S PRISONS TO THE
DOGES' PALACE—THE
MISERY OF THE
CONDEMNED TO THE
POWER OF THE MIGHTY.

THE ISLE OF SAN GIORGIO MAGGIORE FROM THE TOP OF THE BELL TOWER, WHERE THE VIEW OF VENICE AND THE LAGOON IS SUBLIME.

THE PROCURATIE NUOVE, AN IMMENSE ADMINISTRATIVE BUILDING IN THE CLASSICAL STYLE (LATE SIXTEENTH TO EARLY SEVENTEENTH CENTURY), ON THE RIGHT SIDE OF THE BASILICA, AS VIEWED FROM SAINT MARK'S SQUARE.

THE HONAGRIA HOTEL.

THE PALAZZO VENDRAMIN, A CIPRIANI RESIDENCE.

snob seeking luxury, hypochondriac-poet, pleasure-hunting transvestite, salt-water sailor, *commedia dell'arte* character, refined music lover.

Venice is a two-pronged city spanning the Grand Canal that meanders like the river it once was, bordered by the finest of palaces. Here is a broad "boulevard" with no sidewalks, lapping against walls with rings for mooring boats (gondolas used to tie up at the main floor or shop level, where business was conducted). The land extends northward, taking the city with it beyond Saint Mark's and the Palace of the Doges, to the Riva degli Schiavoni where large cruise liners and military vessels still dock. Then toward the Arsenal, seat of the Republic's power, and the gardens—*Giardini*—on the far side of the Via Giuseppe Garibaldi, a wide Napoleonic boulevard (real this time) born of the urban dreams nourished by a man who believed himself master of the world, and leading to a working-class neighborhood of little interest to tourists. The large quays seem to open directly onto the sea, with the Lido tracing a line to the left. In the foreground, long before the pale Gothic façade of the Doges' Palace can be discerned rising in the distance, comes the isle of San Giorgio Maggiore at the end of the Grand Canal, echoing the massive shape of La Salute, Our Lady of Salvation, beside

the customs house, La Dogana, on the tip of the other bank. Here, its far side turned toward the large isle of La Giudecca, is one of the loveliest spots in Venice: the Zattere, or broad western quays that are less crowded than the Riva degli Schiavoni and offer a superb view of the sea and the huge ferries leaving for Greece and Turkey. Continuing on our way, we come to the docks, the Piazzale Roma, the railroad station, and the Grand Canal, which one must cross to go eastward to the other side of the city and its ghetto (the first in Europe), the charming Madonna dell' Orto section, and then the Fondamente Nuove, or new docks, with their tang of sea air and view of ships departing for the isles of San Michele (the cemetery), Burano, Murano, and Torcello. But our circuit of Venice is still not complete: we must pick our way through a maze of little dead-end streets leading to the canals (actually called rios) and canal crossings. We might conclude by returning to Saint Mark's or the Arsenal, or with a boat tour on the Number 5 line, which must be taken in several consecutive laps by those who don't want to tour Murano or the Lido. This will provide an overview of a city that can then be explored in detail

THE RIALTO, THE DOGES' PALACE, THE GRAND CANAL, SAINT MARK'S SQUARE... VENICE CAN SEEM UNREAL AT NIGHT, AND IN FINE WEATHER IT IS HARD TO GO HOME TO BED.

through each of its six sections: Canareggio, San Marco, Castello, Dorsoduro, San Polo, and Santa Croce. Pedestrians can also take a walking tour of the inner city, again on either side of the Grand Canal, following two intersecting itineraries: from the north side of Saint Mark's Square to the Rialto, the monumental central bridge; and from the south side of the Rialto to the Accademia, where another bridge leads back to Saint Mark's. In these crowded, shop-lined streets, between the tourists and natives, Venice lives out its life.

A slender water-taxi made of varnished wood or a serenading gondolier (neither of them cheap), could show you the city, but it would take many days to do it properly—and many nights as well, since Venice is especially lovely at night, with the Grand Canal pitch dark and sometimes empty of boats, mellow lamplight reflecting on the water and the damply glistening ground. Shadowy figures pass by, cats slink along walls, voices dance in the silence of a city disturbed by few engines, water laps against the steps leading to the quays. The water, source of Venice's power and its mystery, also plays a faint music that will yield its secrets—perhaps—only to those willing to listen well.

A SUMMER NIGHT ON THE TERRACE OF THE CIPRIANI HOTEL.

THE PLAIN OF THE PO
RIVER IS VENICE'S
PRODUCE GARDEN.
THE FRUITS,
VEGETABLES, AND
FISH AT THE RIALTO
MARKET SHOULD BE
ADMIRED FIRST THING
IN THE MORNING. A
FEAST FOR THE EYES, A
FRIENDLY ATMOSPHERE,
AND AN OPPORTUNITY
TO USE SOME OF TONI'S
RECIPES.

GRILLED RAZOR CLAMS

Serves 6
3 lbs. razor clams, olive oil,
1 lemon, parsley, pepper

Assemble the clams in bunches and tie or attach with an elastic to keep them from opening. Soak for several hours in cold water. Untie the clams and grill them, a few at a time, over charcoal, or sauté them in a lightly oiled skillet placed over a high heat. Grill them very briefly, in order to preserve their juices. Place the grilled clams on a large serving dish, season with pepper, moisten with the juice of one lemon and a dash of olive oil. Chop the parsley, sprinkle it over the clams, and serve.

TWO TYPICALLY VENETIAN DISHES PREPARED BY TONI.

RISOTTO WITH CUTTLEFISH INK

Serves 6
1 lb. *Vialone Nano* rice,
2 lbs. cuttlefish, 1 onion, 1 clove garlic, ¼ cup olive oil, parsley,
½ cup white wine, 6 cups fish or chicken broth, salt, pepper

Clean, prepare and cook the cuttlefish in the manner described in the recipe for cuttlefish in their ink (see next page). When the wine has been added and the cuttlefish is cooked, add the rice to the pan. Stir for 3 minutes. Slowly add the hot broth, cover, and simmer over low heat until the rice is done

and all the liquid has been absorbed. Add the ink as described in the recipe for cuttlefish in their ink. Season with salt and pepper to taste. As with any risotto, stir vigorously with a wooden spoon during the final minutes of cooking time, adding a few drops of olive oil if needed. (See "Basic Risotto," p. 123).

WATERFOWL WITH POLENTA

Serves 2
1 waterfowl with giblets, ¼ cup olive oil, 1 onion, 1 stalk celery, 1 sprig rosemary, thyme, a few leaves sage, cloves, juniper berries, ½ cup white wine (Tocai type), chicken broth (if necessary), 1 lemon, salt, pepper, 1 tbsp. butter (optional)

The folaga is a migratory waterfowl that winters on the lagoon, where it is hunted like wild duck. If you are not a hunter yourself, you can purchase folaga from the small shop specializing in game located behind the Rialto market. The recipe below is suitable for all dark-fleshed fowl.

Cut off the bird's head and make a shallow incision in the neck. Grasp the flap of skin with a cloth and gently pull it away, removing

CACCIA DELLA BOTTE BY PIETRO LONGHI, CA' REZZONICO MUSEUM.

skin and feathers in a single motion. Cut off wing-tips and feet. Thoroughly clean the interior of the bird, setting aside the giblets. Cut open the gizzard, clean, and chop. Chop the heart and liver. Peel and chop the onion, pare and chop the celery. Split the bird in two lengthwise. Place it in a casserole with the olive oil, vegetables, herbs, spices, and gizzard. Cover and simmer over low heat for 15 minutes, turning occasionally to cook evenly. Add the wine. Continue simmering for about 1 hour, moistening with a little chicken broth if necessary to prevent sticking. When the bird is almost done, add the heart and liver. Add the peel and juice of 1 lemon. Season with salt and pepper from the mill. Just before serving, a little butter may be added to the sauce to thicken it. Vinegar can be substituted for the lemon juice. Serve with polenta.

This dish can also be used as a sauce for *pappardelle*, in which case the bird should be cut into 6 or 7 pieces.

PER RIALTO

GRISSINI (BREAD STICKS) AT HARRY'S BAR.

CUTTLEFISH IN THEIR INK

Serves 6

3 lbs. whole cuttlefish, olive oil, 1 clove garlic, 1 mild onion, 1 stalk celery, 1½ cups dry white wine, ½ cup chopped parsley, 1 bay leaf, 1 cup fish broth, salt, pepper from the mill

Rinse the cuttlefish. Remove the ink sacs and set them aside in a bowl. Remove the skin, eyes, bones, and beaks. Cleanse the interiors and rinse well. Cut the prepared fish into thin slices. Crush the garlic and chop the onion and celery. Place a casserole over low heat. Add the oil, followed by the garlic, onion, and celery. Sauté gently until they are golden. Remove the garlic, and add the cuttlefish, the chopped parsley, and the bay leaf. Add the wine and simmer until it has evaporated. Add the fish broth. Simmer for 15 to 25 minutes, depending on the size of the cuttlefish. Place a strainer over the casserole and fill it with the ink sacs from the bowl. Remove it before the contents of the casserole turn completely black. Season with salt and pepper. If necessary, add a little more fish broth to keep the preparation moist. Serve this dish with white cornmeal polenta.

FRIED SOFT-SHELL CRABS

Serves 6

3 lbs. soft-shell crabs, 2 eggs, flour, 4 tbsps. olive oil, 1 lemon, salt

These tiny soft-shell spider crabs, now raised in captivity, are found only in the lagoon. They are available at the Rialto market during the twice-yearly molting season, in November and in March.

Purchase live soft-shell crabs (*molecche*). Beat the eggs in a large bowl, add the crabs and mix thoroughly. Cover the bowl and place in refrigerator for 1 hour, during which time the live crabs will consume the egg. Remove the crabs from the refrigerator and cut off their claws (the only hard portion). Dredge the trimmed crabs in flour, shaking well to remove the excess. Heat the olive oil in large skillet over a high heat. Sauté the crabs briefly and drain them on absorbent paper. Season with salt. Arrange the crabs on a serving dish and sprinkle them with lemon juice. Serve with polenta, the ideal accompaniment for this dish.

VENETIAN-STYLE SPIDER CRABS

Serves 2

2 medium-sized (¾ lb.) live spider crabs, 1 lemon, extra-virgin olive oil, 1 stalk celery, 1 heart lettuce, salt, pepper from the mill

The spider crab (also called maja squinado*) is in fact a Mediterranean creature, which lives on the* sandy floor of the sea-bed. It is also commonly found in the Adriatic and is a staple of Venetian cuisine.*

Rinse the crabs. Tie the claws of each crab to its body with string. Fill a large pot with water and bring to a rolling boil. Add the crabs and a generous dash of salt. Boil for about 12 minutes. When the crabs are done, remove them from pot and drain them. Open the crabs by pulling the two portions of their body apart. Remove the coral and set it aside. Reserve the hollow half of each shell. Shred the heart of lettuce, the celery, and the crab meat (found mainly in the claws). Chop the coral very finely. Mix all ingredients lightly together and fill the hollow shells with the mixture. Season with a dash of olive oil, a little lemon juice, and pepper. Serve at once.

FISH BROTH

Makes 8 cups of fish broth

2 lbs. fish (go, gurnard, scorpion fish, bass, dory, shellfish claws and shells), 1 medium onion, 2 leeks (white portion only, well rinsed), 1 stalk celery, 4 tbsps. olive oil, 1 cup dry white wine, 8 cups water, juice of ½ lemon, 1 tsp. mixed herbs in cheesecloth bag, 3 bunches parsley, 1 bunch fresh thyme, 1 bay leaf, black pepper, salt

Chop the onion, leeks, and celery into rough pieces. Heat the olive oil in a large pot. Add the vegetables and the fish. Sauté, stirring, until golden. Add the wine, water, lemon juice, bag of herbs, parsley, thyme, bay leaf, and salt and pepper seasoning. Bring the broth to a boil, then skim it. Reduce the heat, partially cover the pot, and simmer for 20 minutes. Strain the cooked broth into a soup tureen, and serve.

THE MURANO
LIGHTHOUSE.

THE GLASSMAKING CITY
OF MURANO IS EASILY
ACCESSIBLE FROM
VENICE BY
VAPORETTO. THE GLASS
KILNS WERE MOVED TO
MURANO IN 1291
BECAUSE OF THE FIRE
HAZARD THEY
REPRESENTED IN THE
CITY OF THE DOGES.

VENICE AND THE ARTS

In contrast to the kingdoms and empires lying beyond its borders, Venice is notable for having cultivated that noblest and most exacting of the arts (since it requires the participation of all): the art of the commonwealth, the Republic. For Venice—outstandingly, more splendidly, and more continuously than any other—has been a realm, a city, of citizens. To be sure, it was not a democracy in which each individual had an equal voice; but the people did play a role in choosing their masters, the doges, through a complex electoral system that (with a helping hand from chance) discouraged dynastic ambitions and intrigue. Despite some inevitable periods of tension, an amazing harmony prevailed. It is thus not surprising that Venice also awarded the arts in general a central place in the life of the city. First, it created between land and sea the loveliest of settings, a backdrop against which life

itself became an art, and beauty a shared value. But it was a beauty firmly based on a sense of craftsmanship, and even technology. These people—who raised their city atop a forest of tree trunks planted in the seabed, invented the gondola, and pioneered the art of glassmaking—had their dreams anchored in reality. They also nourished a taste for festive occasions rooted in a love of life, and a love of communal life. Although it may have stirred anger in the envious, this taste for good living has always been freely shared with outsiders—first with traders from the East and then, increasingly, with visitors attracted solely by its opulent festivities.

Official festivals, conducted according to strict rules confirming the Republic's splendor, were numerous. The *Sensa*, or Marriage of Venice with the Sea celebrated on Ascension Day, was the most ritualized, the most symbolic; but it was more than just an excuse for the *Bucintoro*'s rare appearances. It was also

FARMACIA DELL'ORSO

Campo S. Maria Formosa

THE BEAR, ONCE THE
EMBLEM OF VENETIAN
BOATMEN.

a popular festival, a vast spectacle held in the bay of Saint Mark's, an immense fair swathed in Oriental draperies and silks, at which painters and sculptors were invited to display their works outside the palaces and churches for which they had been executed. The *Sensa* could not be held without a doge and a *Bucintoro*, however, and when the French occupation put an end to the Venetian Republic in 1797, there was no longer anyone left to cast the golden ring into the sea off the coast of the Lido.

In Venice, religion was never austere. Here, as elsewhere, it was taken seriously, of course, but religious festivals were joyous occasions. Every year, the Feast of The Holy Redeemer is still held on the third Sunday in July on the waters of the bay of Saint Mark's and the Giudecca Canal. Although no doubt less elaborate today than in the past, it has retained its role as one of Venice's major festivals.

Boats are still used to construct two floating bridges spanning the Grand Canal and the Giudecca Canal. These provide a route for the faithful to cross over to the Church of The Redeemer (commissioned by the city during the 1576 plague), which stands on the bank opposite the Zattere. In former times, on the eve of the great day, flotillas of elaborately decorated boats used to fill the canals, gliding through a city redolent with the fragrance of roast meats and fowl

THE *BUCINTORO* WAS
THE CEREMONIAL BARGE
OF THE DOGES. TODAY
IT IS HONORED
REGULARLY ON SPECIAL
OCCASIONS WHEN THE
HISTORIC REGATTA
AGAIN EMBARKS ON THE
LAGOON.

served to merry-makers on restaurant tables set out for the occasion beside the main canals. On Palm Sunday, doves with bound feet were let loose from the rafters of a loggia on Saint Mark's, creating an intriguing spectacle as the crowd attempted to catch them for inclusion on the Easter-dinner menu. The traditional meal eaten on Saint Martha's Day once featured sweet-and-sour sole (*el sfogio in saor*), prepared according to a recipe still used today for sardines. On other occasions the staple dish was a cabbage and mutton soup called *castradina*. The doge himself set the tone, appearing at a series of formal banquets, at least some of which were held in public. As many as a hundred guests would be summoned to dine at tables set the night before with such

magnificent artistry that the public was invited to view them. Crystal, china, silverware, flowers, and spun-sugar decorations vied with each other in splendor. Onlookers were asked to leave after the first course had been served. Then, when only the invited guests remained, the entertainment could begin.

The greatest of all Venetian festivals was of course the Carnival, which the records tell us was already popular as far back as 1094. During its golden age, the Carnival of Venice was an extended city-wide bacchanal. It began with the voyage of the doge—amid thousands of glowing lights affixed to the gondolas bobbing up and down in the bay of Saint Mark's—to San Giorgio Maggiore for Midnight Mass at Christmas. From then until Shrove Tuesday, all of Venice became a stage, and

GIANDOMENICO TIEPOLO (1727–1780), *CLOWNS AND TUMBLERS* (DETAIL), CA' REZZONICO MUSEUM. A FRESCO EXECUTED FOR THE VILLA ZIANIGO SATIRIZING EIGHTEENTH-CENTURY VENETIAN SOCIETY.

GIOVANNI BATTISTA BRUSTOLON (1712–1759), AFTER CANALETTO, *VISIT OF THE DOGE TO LA SALUTE*, ENGRAVING, CORRER MUSEUM.

ON THE FEAST OF THE HOLY REDEEMER, A PONTOON BRIDGE IS ERECTED ACROSS LA GIUDECCA CANAL FOR PEDESTRIANS, AS ILLUSTRATED BY JOSEPH HEINTZ THE YOUNGER IN *THE PROCESSION OF THE REDEEMER, CIRCA* 1648.

THE PREMIERE OF GIUSEPPE VERDI'S *LA TRAVIATA* WAS PERFORMED HERE ON MARCH 6TH, 1853.

THE CA' REZZONICO MUSEUM HOLDS A FINE COLLECTION OF WORKS BY PIETRO LONGHI.

GIOVANNI GREVEMBROCH (EIGHTEENTH CENTURY), *MASKED NOBLEMAN WITH SWORD.* WATERCOLOR. CORRER MUSEUM.

the Venetians players in the performance. Citizens of all ranks donned masks and assumed roles in a mad dance no one dreamt of taking seriously. Lights burned late into nights that no longer sought silence. Improvised balls were held in public squares. Crowds thronged the Campo San Stefano and the Piazza San Marco. Coins rang on gaming tables. Convents flung open their doors. Ephemeral romances began and ended. Bull-baiting contests with dogs were organized in squares and palace courtyards.

The Carnival climaxed on the last Tuesday before Lent, when a gigantic pyre, built in front of the Doges' Palace by the winners of an architectural com-petition, was set alight to the accompani-ment of a stunning fireworks display. Sporting events known as the Exploits of Hercules pitted representatives from various sections of the city against one another for the execution of highly com-plex athletic feats. And, of course, the "Angel" leapt from the bell-tower to land at the doge's feet.

On the following day, Ash Wednesday, order was restored and the proper tone set for the Lenten period com-memorating Christ's suffering on the Way of the Cross. Theaters clo-sed their doors and people turned to the less flamboyant plea-sures of music, an art more appro-priate to the devotional mood. Public behavior was tempered by the soothing strains of orchestras and choirs made

ONE OF SAINT MARK'S
MANY TREASURES IS
THIS ANCIENT ROMAN
GOLD AND ENAMEL
CHALICE.

CANDLELIGHT
PROCESSION ON THE
FEAST OF THE *SALUTE*.

up of young girls—most of them pupils from convents. These musicians eventually gained renown throughout Europe, and by the eighteenth century were drawing music lovers to concerts in all seasons, not just in Lent. Venice was a musical city. Adrian Willaert traveled all the way from Flanders to exercise his art there, serving as choirmaster at Saint Mark's, where the architecture of the basilica inspired him to develop an antiphonal form of music (using double choirs) that would later be used extensively. Claudio Monteverdi (1567–1643) held the same post and spent the final thirty years of his life in Venice. The very year of his death he supervised the Venetian première of his opera *L'incoronazione di Poppea* (*The Coronation of Poppea*), one of the greatest works in European musical history. The priest Antonio Vivaldi (1678–1741) served as *maestro di violino* at the newly-built Ospedale della Pietà, a girls' orphanage with a conservatory designed for acoustic quality. It was there, before he turned to secular music, that Vivaldi composed most of his sacred pieces, including a splendid setting of the *Stabat Mater*.

For Venetian art and festivals alike, the distinction between the secular and the profane was far from clear: the latter often lurked behind the former. It is

perhaps this art of the mask, this subtle sleight-of-hand, that accounts for a part of the city's genius. It in any case explains the uniqueness of Venetian painting, which was humane before humanism became fashionable, and sensual before the eighteenth century added a more frivolous note to European morals.

For Venice has traditionally been a feast for the eye rather than the ear. Its great musicians were not specifically Venetian—unlike its painters, to whom we owe a distinctive school extending from the end of the Middle Ages through the Renaissance and the eighteenth century. This was a school remarkable for its humane,

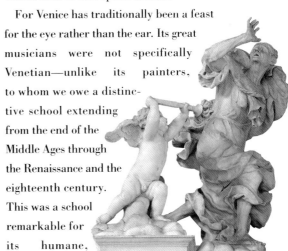

sensual style based on emotion rather than abstraction, and one in which Bellini, Titian, Veronese, Tintoretto, and Tiepolo particularly excelled. The roots of this artistic pre-eminence are perhaps to be found in Byzantium, that city emblematic of a time when both God and the gods had deserted Rome; and in the Orient, toward which Venice had always turned. There, luxuries of a more voluptuous kind were cultivated with no fear of excess or desire to reject the world. The basilica of Saint Mark's, which was erected in the eleventh century to replace an earlier one that had been destroyed by fire, has always stood as the exotic core of a city delighting in its own ostentatious wealth and worldly goods; a city undaunted by frivolous exaggeration. There can be something slightly oppressive about this: a fear of unfilled space, a determination to prevent the soul from engaging in abstract meditation. Saint's Mark's vast façade, its arches and cupolas, extended loggia, pinnacles, opulently gilded marbles and mosaics, and gemencrusted, enameled Altarpiece (the *Pala d'Oro*) combine to make it a peerless monument—the apogee of Orientalism as expressed through Christianity. Parenthetically, the same

obsession with the Orient is reflected by the décor of nearby Florian's—here in an eighteenth-century spirit—although by the time this café opened its doors to Venice's artists and intellectuals, coffee and chocolate (from a very different part of the world) were the newly fashionable luxuries.

The imposing figurative pattern of Saint Mark's mosaic served as a wellspring for Venetian painting up until the nineteenth century. The city's artists—while respecting its original spirit—drew from it and expanded on it, especially during the sixteenth century, at the peak of the Renaissance. The mosaic technique of affixing tiny chips of precious stone onto a plane surface requires an uncomplicated design. In this case, however, the colors against their gold background are resplendent and seemingly eternal. Here is a model that cannot be ignored. But it has also been a

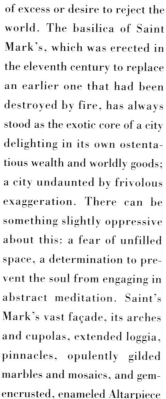

SUPERB MARBLE FLOOR AT THE MARCIANA LIBRARY, OPPOSITE THE DOGES' PALACE.

THE CEILING AT THE PALAZZO PAPADOPOLI IS BY TIEPOLO.

MOSAIC ON ONE OF THE DOMES OF SAINT MARK'S BASILICA. THE OLDEST OF THESE MOSAICS DATES FROM THE TWELFTH CENTURY.

THE MARCIANA LIBRARY HAS A COLLECTION OF 500,000 VOLUMES. IT IS HOUSED IN THE LIBRERIA VECCHIA, A FINE SIXTEENTH-CENTURY BUILDING OPPOSITE THE DOGES' PALACE.

DETAIL FROM THE PENTECOST DOME ON SAINT MARK'S BASILICA.

HARRY'S BAR IS FAMED
FOR ITS CREATIVE
COCKTAILS, ITS
RESTAURANT, AND ITS
ASSOCIATION WITH
ERNEST HEMINGWAY.

THE DANIELI HOTEL
LOBBY.

burden. The Venetian school of painting was able to shed the overwhelming weight of its Byzantine influence only gradually. Giotto (1266–1337), a native of Tuscany, was already bringing a fresh new style to Padua, while Paolo Veneziano (active from 1310 to 1358) continued to practice a gilded, hieratic art, but transferred the nobly religious decorative style from ceilings and walls to altar polyptychs. This pivotal initiative marked the transition from mosaics to paintings, which, although visually more immediate, were as yet unaffected by the turbulence of the Renaissance. Giovanni Bellini (1430–1516) introduced depth and perspective into his work, but did not allow himself to become carried away by this new method of depicting the world. With consummate humility, he used perspective merely as means to create backdrops for his tenderly depicted and expressive personages, transforming the great Bible stories into ordinary incidents of human life.

Bellini's younger contemporary Vittore Carpaccio (1465–1525) was also less than "modern" at a time when Michelangelo and Leonardo da Vinci were already endowing the plastic arts with the breadth and intelligence of a Renaissance philosophy

LA CANTINA DO MORI,
A WELL-KNOWN WINE
BAR.

FLORIAN'S TRADITIONAL
RIVAL ON SAINT MARK'S
SQUARE, THE CAFÉ
QUADRI.

striving to show human beings as masters of the universe. In nine admirable paintings displayed at the little church of San Giorgio degli Schiavoni, Carpaccio demonstrated a keen sense of religious hagiography for his narrative illustration of an exalted spirituality still rooted in the Middle Ages. By contrast, Giorgione (1478–1510), exhibiting a charm comparable to Bellini's, did not shrink from full-blown sensuality.

The next generation stood squarely in the Renaissance—which by this time had spread throughout Europe—but did not become mired in excessive intellectualism. It adopted the humanist conception of human beings as wise and heroic figures in a world structured by perspective, but was not limited by pure reason, and gave full rein in its compositions to movement and color. After first infiltrating a number of churches and palaces, this style of painting—considered quintessentially Venetian by art historians—finally gained a significant foothold behind the noble façade of the Doges' Palace itself. This happened when Titian (*circa* 1488–1576), Tintoretto (1518–1594), and Veronese (1528–1588) were commissioned to redecorate the fire-damaged private apartments of the doge. These painters

WELLS ARE FREQUENTLY
FOUND ON PUBLIC
SQUARES AND IN PALACE
COURTYARDS.

CA' PESARO, MUSEUM
OF MODERN ART (FAR
LEFT, TOP). CAMPO
DIETROIL CIMETERO
(LEFT, TOP).

CORTE BOTERA
(FAR LEFT, BOTTOM).
CA' D'ORO, A FINE
GOTHIC BUILDING
RESTORED IN 1984 AND
HOUSING A MUSEUM
(LEFT, BOTTOM).
THE RED MARBLE WELL
DATES FROM 1428.

COURTYARD OF THE
PALAZZO BARBARO ON
THE CAMPO SAN
STEFANO.

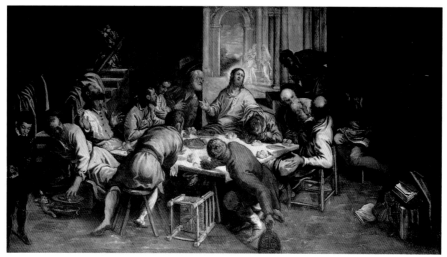

created works of art that stood in audacious and startling contrast with the Byzantine complexity of the basilica next door.

Their heir was Tiepolo (1697–1770), who deployed his joyous spirit, light touch, lifelike subjects and cheerful illumination during the period when Venice was living the final century of its glory.

Pietro Longhi (1702–1785) and Gabriele Bella (1730–1799) were the charming chroniclers of a Venice in which pleasure-seeking and a taste for festive occasions continued to fan the dying embers of the Republic. Later, in the nineteenth and twentieth centuries—first under Austrian occupation and then as part of Italy—Venice was forced to invent new ways to exhibit her charms. The city decided to live life to the full, and to invite the whole world to join in her celebration of life.

Mariano Fortuny y Madrazo (1871–1949), whose life straddled two centuries, embodied the modern destiny of a Venice determined to outwit time. During an era when a few wealthy members of the social elite still maintained the tradition of sumptuous entertainment, this Spaniard from Grenada chose the lagoon as an ideal setting for displaying his sinuous, expansive genius. Fortuny's father, a renowned artist and connoisseur, had imbued him with a taste for fine fabrics, and it is in this realm that he was to shine. As both artist and scientist, he was strongly attracted by the theater, for which he invented a novel system of lighting. It was through his work on stage settings and costumes that

he came to develop the elegant and marvelously colored fabrics that afforded newfound luxury and ease to feminine fashion. One of Fortuny's most famous inventions was the original, patented system of pleating that was later to become his hallmark. The wealthy American heiress Peggy Guggenheim, who transferred her life and her art collection to a palace on the Grand Canal, liked to wear Fortuny gowns for the extravagant parties she organized, and today one can still purchase fabrics signed with the famous designer's name in a small shop near Saint Mark's called V. Trois.

Visitors unable to afford these costly fabrics might like to take home instead some of the exquisite marbled papers that can be found almost everywhere in Venice, but particularly at the shop run by Alberto Valese-Ebru behind the Campo San Stefano or at the Legatoria Piazzesi. There they can choose among pretty notebooks covered with marbled paper in which to keep a diary of their trip, loose sheets for writing letters back home, and a variety of stationery items recalling the fact that Venice is also a city of authors, inhabited by the ghosts of Petrarch and Casanova, Stendhal and Lord Byron, Marcel Proust and Thomas Mann, Ezra Pound and James Hadley Chase.

SCAMPI, A GEM OF
VENETIAN CUISINE, IS
COMBINED WITH
SPAGHETTI TO MAKE
SPAGHETTI WITH SCAMPI
(SEE RECIPE ON RIGHT).

TONI'S "GONDOLA" CANAPÉS

Ingredients for 1 Canapé
(serves 1)
several leaves rocket lettuce,
olive oil, sweet balsamic vinegar,
1 slice bread, 1 fresh scallop in
shell, *fleur de sel* salt, pepper,
lemon, chopped chives,
1 small black Italian truffle
(*tuber melanosporum*)

Wash and dry the rocket leaves,
then dress them with oil and vinegar. Toast the slice of bread and
place it on top of the
salad. Open the scallop,
and carefully remove
the white flesh only.
Rinse the scallop meat,
cut it into thin slices,
and arrange it on the toast. Season with *fleur de sel* salt, pepper,
a dash of olive oil, a drop of lemon
juice, and a few chopped chives.
Grate the truffle into thin slices
and use it to garnish the top of the
canapé.

SPAGHETTI WITH SCAMPI

Serves 6
3 lbs. large scampi,
1 clove garlic, parsley,
1 small red pepper,
2 tbsps. olive oil,
6 tbsps. tomato sauce
(see recipe p. 92), salt,
1½ lbs. uncooked spaghetti,
2 tbsps. grated Parmesan
cheese (optional)

Split the scampi in two lengthwise. Remove the claws and the
sac on either side of the head.
Chop the garlic and the parsley,
and slice the red pepper into thin
strips. Place the olive oil in a
large skillet over a medium heat.
Add the garlic and sauté until
golden (approx. 30 seconds).
Add the prepared scampi, parsley, red pepper and tomato sauce
to the skillet. Season to taste with
salt. Cook for 3 minutes. Remove
the skillet from the heat. Meanwhile, fill a large pot with salted
water and bring to a rolling boil.
Add the spaghetti and cook to
the *al dente* stage. Drain. Add
the cooked spaghetti to the skillet
with the other ingredients. Stir
well over a medium heat for 2
minutes. Pour the contents of the
skillet into a warm serving dish.
Serve at once, accompanied if
desired with a bowl of grated
Parmesan cheese on the side.

VENETIAN-STYLE LIVER

Serves 4
1½ lbs. calves' liver,
2 large onions,
2 tbsps. butter,
¼ cup extra-virgin olive oil,
salt, pepper,
1 tbsp. finely chopped parsley

Cut the onions and liver into thin
slices. Heat most of the butter
and the oil in a skillet over a low
heat. Add the onions and cook
them until golden. Raise the heat
under the skillet to medium, add
the slices of liver and cook for 2
or 3 minutes (to taste), stirring
vigorously. Season with salt and
pepper, transfer to serving
dish and keep warm. Put
the remaining butter in
the hot skillet and let it bubble.
Toss the parsley in the butter for
a few seconds. Sprinkle the fried
parsley over the liver and onions
and serve, accompanied with
polenta.

TRUFFLE
GRATER.

FILLETS OF DORY

Serves 6
6 fillets of dory, flour, 2 eggs,
olive oil, salt, pepper, 2 lemons

Rinse the fillets of dory and wipe
dry. Dredge with flour, shaking
to remove the excess. In a large
bowl, beat the eggs, add salt,
pepper, and the juice of half a
lemon. Dip the floured fillets in
the egg mixture, remove, and
allow to rest for 30 minutes in the
refrigerator. Heat the oil in a
skillet over a medium heat. Add
the fillets and sauté until done,
turning at least once. Serve with
lemon wedges and a green salad.

GALANI, FRITTERS
TRADITIONALLY SERVED
AT CARNIVAL TIME.

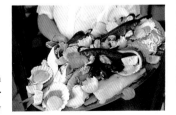

THE DAY'S FRESH
FISH ARE
CUSTOMARILY
DISPLAYED TO
RESTAURANT
DINERS BEFORE
BEING COOKED.
FABULOUS
FRESHNESS!

BURANELLA-STYLE FISH PAPILLOTTES

Serves 2

1 small bass (approx. 1 lb.),
1 mullet (¾ lb.), 2 fresh scampi,
12 clams, 1 egg, 1 tbsp. butter,
1 tbsp. olive oil, 1 tbsp. white
wine, 2 tbsps. tomato sauce
(see recipe p. 92),
rind of 1 lemon, garlic, parsley,
baking parchment

Preheat oven to 425°F. Rinse the clams one at a time under running water to remove the sand. Scale, clean, and rinse the fish. Dredge the fish with flour. Heat the butter and olive oil in a skillet over a medium heat, add the dredged fish and sauté briefly on both sides. Cut a sheet of baking parchment large enough to hold all the ingredients. Place the fish, clams, scampi, the tomato sauce, white wine, and parsley on the sheet, and make into a parcel by folding over the edges and sealing the corners with beaten egg. Place the parcel in a roasting pan and bake in hot oven for 12 to 15 minutes. The parcel will expand in the heat. When fully expanded, the fish is done.

OVEN-BAKED BASS

Serves 2

1 medium-sized bass (approx.
2 lbs.), 1 lb. firm potatoes (Rosevald, Maine), 2 tomatoes, 1 sprig
rosemary, 1 mild onion, 3 tbsps.
olive oil, 2 tbsps. butter,
salt, pepper

Preheat oven to 425°F. Scald and peel the tomatoes. Scale and rinse the bass. Wash, peel, and slice the potatoes. Heat the butter and 2 tablespoons olive oil in a skillet over medium heat. Add the potatoes and sauté for 6 to 7 minutes, turning occasionally. Transfer

the potatoes to a roasting pan and place in the preheated oven. In the skillet, sauté the bass for 3 minutes on each side. Place the sautéed bass on top of the potatoes in the oven. Slice the onion and tomatoes and arrange around the bass. Add the rosemary. Season with salt and pepper, moisten with the remaining olive oil. Bake in hot oven for 10 to 12 minutes.

MANTECATO-STYLE STOCKFISH

Serves 6

2 lbs. air-cured or salt cod,
4 cups extra-virgin olive oil,
4 cups milk, salt, pepper (optional: 2 cloves garlic, 1½ cups
chopped parsley)

This dish is traditionally served on Good Friday. In Italy, it is made with the type of air-cured cod known as stockfish, which can be difficult to find elsewhere. Ordinary salt cod may be substituted, but must be soaked overnight and rinsed several times before being used.

Place the cod in a large pot with the milk. Add enough cold water to cover the cod completely. Bring to the boil, cover, and remove from heat. Allow to rest for 20 minutes. Remove the fish from the pot, reserving the liquid. Skin the fish and remove the bones. Place the fish in a large bowl and use a pestle to reduce it to a purée, while gradually adding olive oil in a thin stream (as for mayonnaise). When the mixture becomes too thick, add enough milk from the pot to obtain a creamy texture. The amount of oil needed will

depend on the quality of the cod. Season to taste with salt and pepper. Serve with freshly-made or baked polenta. (*Optional:* just before serving, add the chopped garlic and parsley. This is delicious but less digestible.)

ZABAGLIONE

Serves 6

6 egg yolks, 6 tbsps. sugar,
1¼ cup Marsala, ½ cup
white wine (*optional:* 1
cup heavy cream)

Venetian bridegrooms are traditionally offered this dish to sustain them during the wedding-night. Zabaglione was originally a beverage. When combined with whipped cream, it becomes a dessert and can also be used as a cake filling.

Place the egg yolks and sugar in a pot with a heavy bottom and blend with an electric beater until the mixture becomes pale, foamy, and forms the "ribbon". Place the pot over low heat and continue beating vigorously, always in the same direction, gradually adding the Marsala and white wine until the mixture thickens. If the zabaglione is to be served as a dessert, allow to cool, whip the heavy cream, and fold in. Zabaglione can also be made in a double-boiler (which takes longer). Beat the mixture in the top half of the double-boiler over boiling water until thick. Remove from heat before the boiling point is reached.

CAPITELLI IS A VERONA
WINE HARVESTED LATE
IN THE FALL. THE
BOTTLE SHOWN IS FROM
AN EXTREMELY GOOD
YEAR, 1990. IDEAL
FOR SIPPING,
ACCOMPANIED BY
BISCUITS.

CHAPTER III

THE LAGOON

THE NORTH BANK OF
VENICE (FONDAMENTA
NUOVE) AS SEEN FROM
THE LAGOON (PREVIOUS
DOUBLE PAGE).

AN ELDERLY GONDOLIER
RELAXING AFTER WORK
ON BURANO, THE
ISLAND OF FISHERMEN
AND LACE-MAKERS.

THE HUGE BUILDING ON
THE ISLE OF LA
GIUDECCA THAT ONCE
HOUSED THE STUCKY
MILL HAS BEEN
CONVERTED INTO A
CULTURAL CENTER,
HOTEL, AND
RESIDENTIAL HOUSING.

Venice rose from the lagoon, and the lagoon has always nourished and protected Venice. This body of water—half-lake, half-sea—is a fertile environment, to which the city built on a group of islands owes its existence. The lagoon is much more than just an extraordinary setting dotted with charming boats. It has its own history and its own life, distinct from that of the city's six sections lying on either side of the Grand Canal. The whole complex does, of course, represent official, administrative Venice: a multifaceted metropolis enclosing the marvelous gem of its ancient center, a modern city on the mainland, a bustling industrial port, and countless islands scattered over a vast stretch of brackish water where inland rivers meet the sea. From another viewpoint, however, Venice would be defined as solely the part that, when you have reached it, can be explored on foot over a multitude of bridges: an extraordinary little town made up of narrow streets and open squares that is self-contained, yet opens onto a placid, rarely stormy lagoon planted with hundreds of wooden piles marking its navigable channels, stretching to infinity in its haze of mist. Facing the bay of the same name, Saint Mark's Square stands on a *piazzetta* framed by two columns, and the Doges' Palace raises its Gothic lace-work under a vast sky. Across the water stands San Giorgio Maggiore, a little island that was home only to cypress tress and Benedictine monks before the Palladian Renaissance added one of its churches to the scene and, in 1951, the Cini Foundation—an active cultural center—established its headquarters there. A few boats cluster in the little marina on the bay of Saint Mark's, beneath the church's bell-tower, and on the other side of the island one need only cross a small canal to reach the larger island of La Giudecca along the southern side of Venice. It was to La Giudecca

THE LIDO IS A NARROW
STRIP OF LAND WITH
TWO CONTRASTING
COASTLINES: ON THE
SOUTH THE BEACH FACES
THE SEA, ON THE NORTH
THE LAGOON.

MURANO'S SANTI MARIA
E DONATO BASILICA,
WITH ITS VENETIAN-
CUM-BYZANTINE STYLE
COLONNADE.

LARGE FISHING NETS
SUBMERGED IN THE
CANALS THAT OPEN INTO
INTO THE LAGOON.

that families banished from the city were once exiled, and, although the island is easily accessible by *vaporetto*, it still seems remote from the city itself. A few palaces were constructed on La Giudecca when there was no more space on the other side of the water, and Palladio designed two large churches there, but it long remained a refuge of country gardens and pure air. Then industry came to the island in the form of the highly visible Stucky flour mill, today under restoration but no longer active. The Fortuny fabric mills, although not open to the public, are still in operation. Another outpost of luxury on the island is the Cipriani hotel—Venice's most elegant—with its large restaurant, park, sea-water swimming pool and private marina. There is also a more modest Cipriani hotel on the island of Torcello: the city's Byzantine cradle, far out in the lagoon, originally settled by refugees from the Barbarian invasion. Once a major city and the seat of a bishopric, Torcello was gradually turned into a malarial swampland by accumulating silt, and its fortunes declined as Venice grew and prospered. Today it is a quiet, sparsely populated city huddled around a very fine cathedral, Santa Maria Assunta, which boasts a noble Romanesque façade and impressive mosaics. Visitors will not want to miss *The Last Judgment*, a mosaic covering the façade of the cathedral and a major masterpiece of

THE FORTUNY FABRIC
MILLS STILL OPERATE ON
LA GIUDECCA.

RESTAURANT
DINING ROOM IN
PORTUGRUARO.

MOST OF THE SMALLER ISLANDS ON THE LAGOON ARE PRIVATELY OWNED.
TORCELLO (ABOVE, TOP LEFT AND BOTTOM RIGHT), WAS A MAJOR BYZANTINE
CITY BEFORE BEING ABANDONED BECAUSE OF ITS MALARIAL SWAMPS.
THE ISLE OF POVEGLIA (ABOVE, TOP RIGHT).

VENETIANS LIKE TO BUY
THEIR FRUITS AND
VEGETABLES FROM
VENDORS PLYING THE
RIO SAN BARNABA
CANAL IN THESE FLAT-
BOTTOMED BOATS.

A WORKSHOP AT THE
FAMOUS MURANO GLASS-
WORKS.

A *MILLEFIORI* GLASS
PAPERWEIGHT
PRODUCED BY THE ALF
GLASSWORKS.

THE ALF GLASSWORKS
ON THE BANKS OF THE
CANALE DEGLI ANGELI.

THE MUSEO VETRARIO,
HOUSED IN A LATE
SEVENTEENTH-CENTURY
PALAZZO, SPECIALIZES IN
GLASS.

Romanesque art. Remote from the bustle of Venice but only three-quarters of an hour away by boat, Torcello is highly appreciated by Venetians as a spot for repose, reverie, and idle strolling.

Three other islands located between Venice and Torcello, readily accessible by vaporetto, also have their own distinctive charm. San Michele, once owned by monks, became a cemetery in 1837 under the Napoleonic regime. The graves of Igor Stravinski, Serge Diaghilev, Ezra Pound, and others attract numerous visitors. Murano is a large village that took over the glassmaking industry in about 1300, when the Venetian government decided that keeping kilns in the middle of town presented too great a fire hazard. Because it was a favored vacation spot for wealthy Venetians, Murano managed to retain its rural character despite the growth of the glass industry. During the sixteenth century it served as a country retreat for Venice's elite, who enjoyed both its cloudless summer weather and the opportunity to stock up on exquisite glassware. Murano quickly achieved a reputation as one of the major glassmaking centers in Europe, exporting most of its production. It was already sending out its lovely, richly hued opaque glass beads all over the world—and the world was already peering into its mirrors—

LYING BENEATH ITS
BELL-TOWER (LA
TORRE), THE CENTER
OF BURANO IS THAT OF
A LIVING, THRIVING
VILLAGE.

le delizie di
Burano
PALMISANO LUIGI
pasticceria dal 1926

A LABEL FROM THE
CAKES THAT ARE A
BURANO SPECIALTY.

when the advent of the Renaissance gave the industry new impetus. Technical experimentation led to important discoveries in glassmaking that raised Murano to the rank of pace-setter in the field. The Museum of Glass is proof that this reputation was well-earned, but today it is wise to avoid the souvenir trinkets totally unrelated to an honorable tradition that some craftsmen, fortunately, are perpetuating: one with abiding appeal to the contemporary artists who have raised glassmaking to the status of a full-fledged art.

The island of Burano owes its fame to the development of lace-making during the sixteenth century, at a time when this craft was not widely practiced elsewhere. A charming legend attributes the origin of this feminine craft to the queen of the mermaids, who is said to have woven a wedding dress from sea-foam for a young bride whose faithful beloved turned a deaf ear to the sirens' alluring song. More prosaically, Burano owes its fame to the invention of the rose-point stitch, or *Point de Venise*, and to the dedicated women whose handiwork conquered all of Europe. Imitations inevitably followed, however, led by those from France's Royal Lace Manufactory founded during the eighteenth century. Venetian lace has survived the intervening centuries, but only with great difficulty. A few women still practice the craft, despite strong competition from the crude imitations of dubious origin that fool so many unwary tourists. Today most people visit Burano to admire the colorful houses lining

THE DAY'S MENU AT THE
TRATTORIA BUSA ALLA
TORRE ON MURANO.

COLOR IS THE
HALLMARK OF BURANO,
A CHARMING LITTLE
VILLAGE WHERE THE
HOUSES ARE
TRADITIONALLY
PAINTED IN VIVID HUES.

narrow canals where fishermen moor their boats. The vivid yellows, ochers, blues, greens, pinks, and purples covering the walls of these houses is usually applied by the occupants themselves, who seem to have an unfailing instinct for the overall harmony that painters and photographers find so appealing.

The Lido is a long, narrow island separating the lagoon from the sea. On the Adriatic side it has a fine sandy beach that during La Mostra—the annual Venice film festival—attracts hordes of starlets and paparazzi. On the Lido, a great resort born of the early twentieth century's taste for luxury, cars are allowed. They are brought in by

THE GREEN CRAB
BREEDS IN THE OPEN
SEA, BUT MIGRATES TO
THE LAGOON.

ferry and are used to drive celebrities to their hotels, or simply to cruise a shoreline equipped with an incalculable number of beach cabanas. The first Mostra was held in 1932, and ever since it has provided fodder for mass-circulation magazines all over the world. Festival prize-winners over the past thirty years include directors such as Louis Malle, Akira Kurosawa, Luchino Visconti, and Wim Wenders. The Golden Lion, the festival's highest award, is copied from the royal lion of Saint Mark's, the emblem of Venice. The urban luxury of this eight-mile long island diminishes

FISHNETS ARE MENDED
BY HAND.

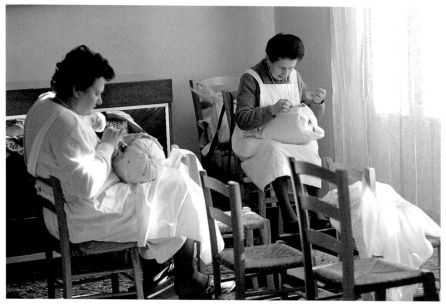

the farther you get from the pier where boats from Venice dock, until finally you reach the ferry connecting it with the next island—poorer, more working-class, almost stark—where the village of Pellestrina faces Chioggia, a large fishing port at the end of the lagoon that serves as the southern gateway to Venezia.

The lagoon has always been a vast hunting-and-fishing ground for Venice. Although threatened by tidal variations and the city's expanding population, it is still a highly distinctive and remarkably well-preserved ecological environment. Fed by various rivers, it resembles a large lake between land and sea. Protected by a sand barrier built up over the centuries by shifting currents, it is accessible through navigable channels at three points: the Lido, Malamocco, and Chioggia. A number of more or less deep channels make it possible to cross the lagoon by boat, but only vessels with extremely flat keels can venture into the areas of shallow water, where the land rises almost to the surface. As the natural habitat of various species of birds, the lagoon is a rich source of game for hunters. Hunting is an ancient Venetian sport, and some wealthy families have constructed quite elaborate hunting lodges on the lagoon's smaller islands. Old paintings often depict marksmen and archers, and it should come as no surprise to learn that wild duck is a favorite Venetian delicacy. Bird-watchers can also

THE SCUOLA DEI MERLETTI, A NEARBY MUSEUM THAT DISPLAYS MAGNIFICENT ANTIQUE LACE.

LACE-MAKING TOOLS.

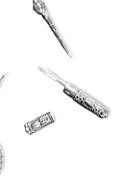

SHOPS OFTEN DISPLAY FACTORY-MADE LACE PRODUCED FAR FROM VENICE.

"TOMBOLO" LACE, A
BOBBIN TYPE
EXTREMELY
POPULAR WITH
TOURISTS.

MOORING IN FRONT OF
A PALACE ON THE
GRAND CANAL.

THE HOTEL DES BAINS (TOP LEFT).

THE HOTEL EXCELSIOR (TOP RIGHT).

THE HOTEL EXCELSIOR BEACH (BOTTOM LEFT).

THE BAGNO DA PAOLINO BEACH CABANAS (BOTTOM RIGHT).

observe the habits of the little egret, bearded titmouse, reed bunting, and reed warbler. The lagoon is by no means a natural wilderness, however. Many of its marshes and tiny islands have been taken over for use as farmland, their crops of vegetables and fruits transported by boat to feed the population of Venice. More remarkable still are the *valli da pesca*, structures built on bulkheads that trap the fish entering the lagoon from the sea. Eels, gilt-head bream and sea bass are the most frequent visitors. Once they have been trapped, they are raised to maturity for market.

Various types of nets are also used on the lagoon by traditional fisherman. The largest boats set out to sea from Chioggia and Malamocco. Venetian cuisine is rich in iodine, provided by a diet of native squill-fish, sardines (prepared in *saor*, a sweet-sour dressing), sole, green crabs, mussels, and squid. Squid ink is used locally to add a distinctive touch to spaghetti or, even better, to risotto. The Venetian diet is, perhaps surprisingly, based more on rice than on pasta (due to the proximity of the river Po and its rice fields), but in fact, Venice is most of all associated with polenta, a type of cornmeal that is used to make a creamy purée but can also be shaped into squares and baked or grilled.

THE LAGOON IS A
WORLD APART, WHERE
THE CROWDS AND
TREASURES OF VENICE
ARE FORGOTTEN.
FISHERMEN, COMPETING
WITH FLOCKS OF BIRDS,
WORK FROM TINY
ISLANDS.

SARDINES ARE
ABUNDANT IN THE
ADRIATIC AND HAVE
LONG BEEN RELISHED BY
THE VENETIANS, WHO
PREPARE THEM IN AN
ORIGINAL MARINADE
CALLED *SAOR*.

FISH SOUP

Serves 4

7 tbsps. olive oil, 2 medium onions, 2 stalks celery, 1 carrot, 1 medium tomato, 2 cups dry white wine, 8 cups hot water, 1 *peperoncino*, 1 bay leaf, 1½ lbs. go (or small flounder-type fish), flour for dredging, 1 bunch fresh rosemary, 1 bunch fresh thyme, 3 sprigs parsley, 1 clove garlic, salt, pepper from the mill

Each region of Italy has its own recipe for fish soup, prepared with the species available locally. The go is a small fish native to the Venetian lagoon that should be purchased live. This recipe is also suitable for fish broth or court bouillon.

Finely chop the celery, onions, and carrot. Scald and peel the tomato. Heat 3 tbsps. olive oil in a large pot over low heat. Add the celery, onions, and carrot to the hot oil and sauté, stirring, for 5 minutes. Add the tomato and cook for 1 minute more. Add the wine, bring to a boil and cook for 3 minutes, stirring continuously. Add the hot water, *peperoncino*, and bay leaf. Season with salt and pepper. Return to the boil. Reduce heat to very low and simmer for 20 minutes. Season the fish with salt and pepper, dredge lightly with the flour. Heat 3 tbsps. olive oil in a large skillet and brown the fish briefly on both sides. Add the browned fish to the ingredients in the pot and continue simmering. Chop the rosemary, thyme, parsley, and garlic. Add to the soup with 1 tbsp. olive oil. Simmer for 3 minutes, stirring to mix well. Season to taste and serve immediately.

In Venice, fish soup is served with pieces of whole fish in it. This soup can also be made with scorpion fish, angler, or scampi.

SQUILL FROM THE LAGOON

Serves 4

2½ lbs. squill, parsley, 1 clove garlic, salt, pepper, 1 lemon, olive oil

This dish is traditionally served on Saint Catherine's Day (November 25), since squill are at their best during the month of November.

Bring a large pot of salted water to a rolling boil. Add the squill, return to the boiling point, and cook 3 to 4 minutes. Remove fish to a strainer and cool slightly by rinsing with a little cold water. Place the squill on a flat surface and use kitchen shears to cut open on either side, working from tail to head. Grasp the tail and pull off the shell in a single movement. Place the shelled squill on a serving platter. Chop the parsley and sprinkle over the fish. Season with salt, pepper, and a dash of olive oil. Cut the garlic clove into thin slices and add at the last minute. Cover the platter and allow to cool until lukewarm. Serve with lemon wedges. The fish broth can be used for making fish soup or risotto.

MARINATED SARDINES

Serves 6

The marinade: ¼ cup olive oil, 2 mild onions, 3 bay leaves, ½ cup white-wine vinegar,
The sardines: 18 fresh sardines, flour, ½ cup olive oil, black pepper, salt

The marinade

Cut the onions into thin slices. Heat the olive in a skillet over a medium heat. Add the onions and bay leaves. Cook, stirring, for 15 to 20 minutes. The onions should be translucent but not golden. Add the vinegar and boil for a few minutes, blending thoroughly, until a thin sauce is obtained. Remove skillet from heat and set aside.

GARLIC HAS BEEN A STAPLE OF MEDITERRANEAN CUISINE SINCE THE DAWN OF TIME. IT OWES ITS TASTE AND FRAGRANCE TO AN ESSENTIAL OIL CALLED ALLIUM. GARLIC IS AT ITS BEST FROM JUNE TO SEPTEMBER.

The sardines

Scale, clean, and rinse the sardines. Split them open lengthwise and place on absorbent paper to dry. Season with salt, dredge with flour. Shake to remove excess flour. Heat the olive oil in a skillet and sauté the sardines briefly (2 minutes on each side) over high heat. Drain the browned sardines on absorbent paper.

Pour one-third of the marinade into a porcelain terrine, season with pepper, and add 9 of the sardines in an even layer. Add the second third of the marinade, season with pepper. Add the remaining sardines and cover with the remaining third of the marinade. Allow to rest for several hours. Serve.

This dish originated in the fourteenth century and was served on gondolas on the eve of the Feast of the Redeemer, the third Saturday in July.

SAINT ERASMUS ARTICHOKES

Serves 4

12 Italian dwarf artichokes (known in Venice as *castraure*), 1 lemon, ¼ cup extra-virgin olive oil, 1 bunch parsley, salt, pepper

In Venice these artichokes are often sold already trimmed. If untrimmed, remove the tough outer leaves and cut the stem to a length of about 2 inches. Rotate a paring knife in a circular motion around the tips of the remaining leaves, trimming them evenly to a length of

about 2 inches. Sprinkle with lemon juice and rinse in a bowl of water and lemon juice in order to prevent the cut tips of the leaves from darkening. Remove the artichokes from the water, wipe dry, and split in half. Heat the olive oil in a large skillet over medium heat and sauté the artichokes on all sides for 8 minutes. Chop the parsley and add. When done, season with salt and pepper. Place in a serving dish, cover, and allow to cool. When lukewarm, add a dash of olive oil and serve.

SHRIMP WITH POLENTA

Serves 2

½ lb. live shrimp (called *schie* in Venice), flour, oil for deep-frying (any type resistant to high temperatures), salt, pepper

These tiny gray shrimp (similar to those found in Brittany and Normandy) turn pink when cooked. They are eaten whole.

Place the shrimp in a large bowl. Season with salt and pepper, stir. Cover the bowl to prevent the live shrimp from escaping. When ready to cook, remove cover and dredge the shrimp thoroughly with flour. Shake in a large strainer to remove excess flour. Heat the oil in a deep-fat fryer until very hot. Add the shrimp and fry

until they turn pink, approximately 3 to 4 minutes. Remove and drain on absorbent paper. Serve with polenta.

VENETIAN-STYLE DOUGHNUTS

Serves 6

½ cup Grappa, ½ cup Corinth raisins, 2 tbsps. yeast, ¼ cup lukewarm water, 2 cups pastry flour, 6 tbsps. sugar, 2 eggs, 1 cup milk, 1 tsp. vanilla, grated peel of 1 lemon, pinch of cinnamon, pinch of salt, oil for frying (any type resistant to high temperatures), additional sugar for dusting the finished pastries

Soak the raisins in the Grappa. Set aside. In a large bowl, dissolve the yeast in the lukewarm water. When the yeast is dissolved (it will foam slightly), add the sugar, milk, and eggs. Whisk to mix thoroughly. Add the raisins and Grappa, grated lemon peel, cinnamon, and salt. Whisk. Add the flour gradually, stirring with a wooden spoon and then kneading until the dough is smooth and firm. Add more flour if necessary. Form the dough into a ball, return to bowl, cover with clean cloth, and allow to rise in a warm place until it has doubled in bulk (5 hours). Turn the dough out onto a floured board, punch down, and knead

until smooth. Place a skillet over high heat and fill to a depth of 1–2 inches with the oil. When the oil is hot, use a spoon to form small rounds of dough, pushing them off the spoon one by one into the oil. Fry them until dark golden on both sides, turning once or twice and keeping them separate. Use a skimmer to remove the cooked rounds from the skillet, drain on absorbent paper, and dust with sugar. Serve while still hot.

THE DWARF ARTICHOKES
KNOWN AS *CASTRAURE*
ARE USUALLY SOLD WITH
THEIR STEMS AND
TOUGH OUTER LEAVES
ALREADY TRIMMED.
TO PREPARE, SAUTÉ IN
A SKILLET.

CHAPTER IV

THE DOLOMITES

RELAXING AT CORTINA
D'AMPEZZO.

CORTINA D'AMPEZZO.
LYING AT 4,000 FT.,
THIS IS THE MOST
FAMOUS SKI RESORT IN
ITALY.

EROSION HAS SCULPTED
BIZARRE SHAPES IN THE
DOLOMITES, THE
MOUNTAIN RANGE THAT
DOMINATES VENEZIA
AND THAT HAS BEEN A
WINTER AND SUMMER
FAVORITE WITH HIKERS,
MOUNTAIN-CLIMBERS,
AND SKIERS EVER SINCE
THE NINETEENTH
CENTURY.

In dramatic contrast with the lagoon to its east, northern Venezia is bordered by the Alps. However, this section of the Alpine range, looming over north-eastern Italy on its frontier with Austria, is different from the rest. The Dolomites, named after the French geologist Déodat de Gratet de Dolomieu, have a unique beauty reflecting a topography that is both sharp and rounded, and displaying rich color contrasts of gold and purple, pink and orange. Dolomitic rock, which is probably petrified sea-coral, is an easily eroded blend of calcium and magnesium. This accounts for the strange formations shaped like organ pipes and crumbling towers that rise above its vast plateaus. These are at their most spectacular in summertime, and are much appreciated by hikers and rock-climbing mountaineers. But during the winter months, Mount Marmolada (which rises to an altitude of almost 11,000 feet) is a favored haunt of skiers, who can choose from among the many resorts located in this mountainous region divided between Venezia and the Trentino. No one knows exactly how long these slopes have been inhabited. The local population falls into two distinct groups. The oldest is made up of those whose native tongue is Ladin, a Romance language that has survived here, in Friuli, and in the Grisons region of Switzerland. The other group has its roots in the Germanic countries, whose customs and language it has preserved. The sixty-mile long Dolomite highway (*Strada delle Dolomiti*), half of which lies in Venezia, spans the Dolomite range from Cortina d'Ampezzo to Bolzano, offering a succession of spectacular views along the way. The highway runs along the foot of the Toffane massif (whose peaks are almost as high as Mount Marmolada) from Cortina, Italy's most famous ski resort, then wends upward to an altitude of over 6,500 feet at the Passo di Falzarego, snakes downward below the ruined fortified castle

IL PIAVE IN CONCA
BELLUNO. THE PIAVE
RIVER FLOWS FROM
UPPER VENEZIA PAST
BELLUNO, EAST OF
CORTINA D'AMPEZZO,
MAKES A WIDE BEND,
AND EMPTIES INTO THE
ADRIATIC JUST NORTH
OF THE VENETIAN
LAGOON (PREVIOUS
DOUBLE PAGE).

CHURCH WITH AN ONION
DOME, A SOUVENIR OF
THE AUSTRO-
HUNGARIAN
OCCUPATION.

of Andraz to the valley of Cordevole, and turns upward once more toward Arabba, a base for hikers. Next come the Passo di Campolongo, and the Passo del Pordoi—a mountain pass lying at an altitude of 7,350 feet that crosses the Venezia border into Trentino–Upper Adige. On the way, travelers might be tempted to ride in one of the several cable cars serving Lagazuoi Piccolo—where one can dine at an altitude of 9,000 feet—and Porta Vescovo, 650 feet lower, the departure point for climbs up Mount Marmolada. But it would be a shame to stop there, and not to drive on to Vigo di Fassa, to the Passo di Costalunga, to Lake Carezza, Nova Levante, Ponte Nova, the Ega valley, and, last but not least, Bolzano—a village displaying an amazing blend of stucco, glass-enclosed balconies, and façades painted in the Austrian style, combined with Italianate courtyards and terraces. Visitors will be intrigued by the Germanic architecture of the churches in some of these villages: a shingled roof, an onion dome resting on a kind of flattened sphere, and six ribs rising to a slender spire topped by a crucifix. These villages also have Germanic names—Karersee, Welschnofen, Birchabruck, Deutschnofen, Eggen Tal, Kardaun, and

INTERIOR OF THE ANTIQUES SHOP IN DOSOLEDO OWNED BY RITA AND ALESSIO SACCO.

CHEESE-MAKING IN TAMBRE D'ALPAGO.

THE CHARM OF A SNOWY WINTER LANDSCAPE.

so on. In the valley of the Zoldo (Valzoldana), the villages of Forno di Zoldo, Fornesighe, and Zoppe di Cadore also boast what is unquestionably a Tyrolean style of building, with their wooden chalets built on stone foundations. Some people might want to hike up the mountains and stop overnight in an Alpine hut. Many of the trails are blazed, and a few (the *vie ferrate*) also have metal handrails—although climbers should be properly equipped before starting out. And, who could resist lingering on the shores of Lake Misurina or Lake Alleghe? Who could resist the temptation, on a beautiful day, to spend long

A CLASSIC POLENTA BASIN. IN THE REMOTE MOUNTAINOUS AREAS, AWAY FROM THE BUSTLE OF THE PLAIN, MANY OF THE TRADITIONAL WAYS HAVE BEEN MAINTAINED.

A SIGN OUTSIDE THE
SHOP OWNED BY RITA
AND ALESSIO SACCO IN
DOSOLEDO GIVES A
FORETASTE OF THE
REGIONAL TREASURES
WITHIN.

THE SHOP RUN BY IMMO
RED, AN ANTIQUES
DEALER IN CORTINA
D'AMPEZZO.

AN ARTIFICIAL LAKE IN
THE VAL DI ZOLDO.
ALTHOUGH THE
DOLOMITES HAVE BEEN
LOGGED FOR CENTURIES,
THEY ARE STILL HEAVILY
FORESTED WITH LARCH,
SPRUCE, PINE, AND FIR.

THE BOSCO DEL CONSIGLIO, EAST OF BELLUNO. ALTHOUGH EXTENSIVELY LOGGED BY THE VENETIANS, THE FOREST HAS RETAINED ALL OF ITS CHARM.

THE MOUNTAINOUS TOPOGRAPHY OF THE DOLOMITES IS DOTTED WITH NUMEROUS LAKES.

moments admiring the flowers, discovering the pink saponaria, the yellow cinquefoil, the blue gentian or the red lily? And who would not feel their heart beat a little faster at the unexpected sight of a chamois, a deer or some other wild animal? Much of the wood that was used for the piles driven into the shifting sands under the Venetian lagoon comes from the Dolomites, particularly from the Pieve di Cadore region on the road rising to Cortina d'Ampezzo from Belluno. Timber (fir, pine, larch, spruce) is still an important resource in these mountains, where farmsteads have become rare. Today, however, tourism is the major industry in this famous area, and Cortina is its most fashionable resort.

Cortina, an elegant Alpine town which was popularized by nineteenth-century British travelers, is strategically located in a sunny hollow surrounded by tall mountain peaks. The town's wooden chalets have not yet been replaced by modern concrete buildings, and some 60 miles of ski trails are available to those who have not come solely to see and be seen, shop, and stuff themselves on *casunzei*, a kind of ravioli. Three museums add a cultural touch to the thrill of winter sports.

HERDS OF DEER ROAM THE DOLOMITES, WHERE THEY CAN ALWAYS SEEK REFUGE IN THE VAST DOLOMITES NATIONAL PARK.

THE CASA VALMASSI IN
DOMEGGE DI CADORE.

The first displays an interesting collection of fossils; the second illustrates the history of the region, and the third offers a fine collection of modern art featuring Giorgio de Chirico's bizarre compositions.

Ski-lifts and cable cars take skiers and visitors from Cortina to the Forcella Staunies (nearly 10,000 feet high), to the other peaks rising around the small town, and to the fabulous viewpoints and broad trails of the Cristallo range. Another popular excursion from Cortina, especially during the summer months, is a tour of the Cadore, an appealing stretch of Alpine meadowland and charming villages tucked among imposing mountain peaks (including Mount Antelao, which has an altitude of 10,700 feet). Visitors to Pieve di Cadore can tour the house in which Titian was born, a fine example of the typical dolomite wooden chalet style. The house contains a few drawings by this greatest of all Venetian painters, and the village church displays a self-portrait in which "Saint" Titian and Saint Andrew are shown worshiping a Madonna and Child. Near Pieve, in Tai Cadore, a small museum that specializes in eye-glasses displays one of the region's traditional crafts through a number of fine antique specimens: opera glasses—the forerunners of binoculars, and used no doubt to gain a closer view of the stage at Venice's La Fenice theater—lorgnettes, aristocratic

THE MAIN SQUARE IN
PIEVE DI CADORE.

BELLUNO,
BIRTHPLACE OF
DINO BUZZATI
(1906–1972),
A MAJOR ITALIAN
WRITER.

monocles, *pinces-nez*, and other optical instruments.

The southern gateway to the Dolomites is Belluno. This old Roman city was built at the strategic junction of the Ardo and Piave rivers—a location that was exploited by Massena when he led his French troops to a decisive victory over the Austrians. The center of the old city is filled with Renaissance and baroque buildings. Construction of the Duomo (cathedral) began at the beginning of the sixteenth century, but the building was never fully completed. It is dominated by a bell-tower that dates from the mid-seventeenth-century. Adding to the charm of the cathedral's interior, which is built out of dolomitic stone, is a fine collection of paintings and sculptures. The fifteenth-century Palazzo dei Rettori (which stands on the cathedral square) boasts a Renaissance façade adorned with Venetian-style arcades and baroque sculptures. This little town in the Piave valley, already mountainous at an altitude of some 1,300 feet, is an ideal base from which to explore the Dolomites. Good hiking trails lead to Mount Serva, Mount Schiara, Lake Santa Croce, and the Dolomites National Park at Belluno—a protected area that is home to some very rare species of flora and fauna.

A back road running through the Cordevole valley climbs up into the Dolomites as far as Mount Marmolada.

TITIAN, *VENERE ALLO SPECCHIO* (VENUS AT THE LOOKING-GLASS), CA' D'ORO, VENICE.

PIEVE DI CADORE IS A PRETTY MOUNTAIN VILLAGE LYING BETWEEN 2,300 AND 3,250 FT. TITIAN WAS BORN THERE, IN A CHALET THAT IS TODAY A MUSEUM.

From there one can skirt around the foot of the mountain, on either side, and rejoin the main Dolomites highway. In summer the road eastward to the superb Sottoguda gorges is open.

On the road from Treviso to Bolzano, the city of Feltre (south of Belluno) is notable for its medieval ramparts and its fine Renaissance manor houses, some of which are decorated with frescos. Carlo Goldoni's first play was performed in Feltre in 1729, at a time when the city was still under the domination of

STATUE OF TITIAN IN PIEVE DI CADORE.

THE PALAZZO DEI
RETTORI WAS BUILT AT
THE END OF THE
FIFTEENTH
CENTURY ON THE
PIAZZA DEL DUOMO
IN BELLUNO, A SMALL
TOWN NESTLED AT
THE FOOT OF THE
MOUNTAINS.

THE PIAZZA MAGGIORE
IN FELTRE IS
DOMINATED BY THE
CROSS OF SAINT MARK,
A REFLECTION OF THE
VENETIAN INFLUENCE.
THE ARCADES OF THE
PALAZZO DELLA
RAGIONE WERE
DESIGNED BY PALLADIO.

Venice—as witnessed by the lion of Saint Mark standing proudly above the Piazza Maggiore. The play was performed in the Palazzo della Ragione, which owes its imposing arcades to Andrea Palladio. A few steps away is the Palazzo del Monte di Pietà, in which the Galleria Rizzarda displays one of the finest collections of wrought iron in the world.

Another of the province's major cities on the road from Treviso to Belluno is Vittorio Veneto. This town was formed by the nineteenth-century merger of two industrialized villages, Serravalle and Ceneda. The first village had forges that specialized in making steel blades for swords, and the second had bronze foundries for casting bells. Vittorio Veneto still bears the physical marks of these trades, and you would be tempted to give the town a miss if you did not know that its two picturesque old village centers have survived, and that each has a bit of history worth stopping for—not in connection with industry but in the field of art.

In the Ceneda ghetto, in 1749, a son named Emmanuele Conegliano was born to a family that had converted to Catholicism. Under the name Lorenzo da Ponte, he wrote the librettos for some of Mozart's most famous operas, including *Don Giovanni*. A little over two centuries later, Franco Zeffirelli filmed several scenes from his *Romeo and Juliet* in the old town of Serravalle.

THE PALAZZO DELLE REGOLE AT CORTINA D'AMPEZZO.

THE PONTE DEGLI ALPINI IN BASSANO DEL GRAPPA. THIS COVERED WOODEN BRIDGE WAS BUILT BY PALLADIO IN 1569.

FAGIOLI, A VARIETY OF
BEANS GROWN AND
DRIED IN THE REGION,
ARE USED FOR
PREPARING EXCELLENT
SOUPS AND SALADS.
FAGIOLI SEEDS ARE
SOWN ALONG NEW ROWS
OF CORN WHICH, AS
THEY GROW, SERVE AS
STAKES FOR THE
BEANSTALKS. THE
BEANS ARE HARVESTED
JUST BEFORE THE CORN,
IN JUNE. *FAGIOLI* AND
FAGIOLINI ARE KISSING
COUSINS.

VENETIAN-STYLE SAUSAGE

Serves 6

1 *Sopressa* sausage, wine vinegar

Sopressa is a thick sausage 5 to 6 inches in diameter. Cut it into thick slices to prevent crumbling. Brown the slices on both sides in an ungreased skillet. Transfer to a serving dish and deglaze the skillet with wine vinegar. Pour the pan juices over the sausage, and serve with polenta and salad in season.

GRILLED CEPS

Serves 2

1 lb. cep-type mushrooms, olive oil, salt, pepper (*optional*: chopped parsley, chopped garlic)

Select very fresh mushrooms (preferably gathered from an oak forest; avoid those with moss under the stems, since they are less fresh). Gently clean the mushrooms with a damp cloth. Cut off the stems and set aside for using later in broth or risotto. Smear the mushroom caps with olive oil, place on a double-sided fold-over grill and lock firmly in place. Grill over a charcoal fire for several minutes on one side, then turn and grill

the other side. Remove from fire, season with salt, pepper, a dash of olive oil and, if desired, the chopped parsley and garlic.

HARICOT BEAN SOUP

Serves 4

1 generous cup dried haricot beans, 8 cups water, 1 onion, 2 cloves, 1 small carrot, 1 stalk celery, 1 tomato, 1 bay leaf, 4 tbsps. small pasta (or tagliatelle noodles broken into small pieces), 1 small bunch basil, olive oil, Parmesan cheese, salt, pepper

The best beans for this soup are the Lamon or Borlotti variety. Soak the dried beans overnight in cold unsalted water to cover. Drain them and place them in a large soup pot with 8 cups cold unsalted water. Peel the onion and stud it with the 2 cloves. Scrape and slice the carrot and the celery. Scald and skin the tomato, remove the seeds. Add the vegetables and bay leaf to the soup pot. Bring the contents of the pot to the boil, lower the heat, and simmer for 2 hours (for beans harvested during the year; longer for older beans). Add water if needed during cooking. When the beans are done, fill a soup ladle with the

cooked vegetables, place them in a food mill, and grind back into the soup. The puréed vegetables will act as a thickener. Add the pasta, bring to a boil, and cook until the pasta is done. Add chopped basil leaves, a dash of olive oil and season with salt and pepper. Serve with a bowl of grated Parmesan cheese on the side. This soup may also be served cold with sautéed bacon bits and grilled polenta. In this case, omit the pasta.

RISOTTO WITH CEPS

Serves 6

2 lbs. cep-type mushrooms, 4 tbsps. olive oil, 1 onion, 2 cups round rice, 4 cups chicken or vegetable broth, salt, pepper, 2 tbsps. butter, 1 bunch parsley, ½ cup grated Parmesan cheese

Rinse the mushrooms briefly and dry on absorbent paper. Remove the stems. Peel and slice the caps. Sauté the mushroom caps in the olive oil until they have wilted. Set them aside in a bowl. Peel and chop the onion, and sauté gently in a casserole before adding the rice and broth. (The peel and stems of the mushrooms may be simmered in water for about 15 minutes, and the cooking water added to the broth for additional flavor.) Simmer until the rice has absorbed all the liquid, adding more broth if necessary during cooking to prevent sticking. Add the mushrooms, season with salt

and pepper, dot with butter, sprinkle with chopped parsley, and serve with grated Parmesan. This risotto will be thicker than risotto made with vegetables.

POLENTA

Serves 6
2 cups cornmeal, 6 cups water,
1 tbsp. salt

Venetian polenta is traditionally made with white cornmeal, which was first imported from Mexico in the seventeenth century. It is still sold under the name granoturco,

a reflection of the Ottoman-Turk influence. The export of white cornmeal is prohibited. This freshly milled meal must be stored in the refrigerator. Polenta made outside Italy is usually yellow.

Place the water and salt in a large copper pot or traditional heavy Italian-style *caldiera*. Bring to a rolling boil over high heat. Sprinkle the corn meal over the boiling water, stirring vigorously with a wire whisk to prevent the formation of lumps. When blended, reduce heat and cover. Stir occasionally with a wooden spoon until the polenta is done. This is easier than the traditional method of stirring the polenta continuously with a wooden spoon for 45 minutes.

When the polenta has thickened, pour it onto a large plate. Serve immediately, or allow to cool, remove from the plate, slice, and brown under the grill.

BIGOLI IN SAUCE

Serves 4
1 lb. Bigoli, 1 large mild onion, 2 tbsps. olive oil, 3 oz. salted anchovies or sardines, 1 bunch parsley, salt, pepper

A traditional recipe, served on Good Friday. Bigoli is a type of spaghetti made by hand from whole-wheat flour.

Bring a large pot of salted water to the boil, add the Bigoli and cook until done. Meanwhile, slice the onion and chop the parsley. Heat the olive oil in a skillet over low heat. Add the sliced onion and cook until soft. Remove pan from fire. Mash the anchovies or sardines with a fork and add to the onion. Add the parsley. When the Bigoli are cooked, drain and add to the other ingredients. Simmer over low heat for 2 minutes. Season with salt and pepper, transfer to a warm serving dish and serve.

TOMATO SAUCE

6 fresh tomatoes (or 1 large can Italian plum tomatoes), 1 small

red pepper, 1 onion, 4 tbsps. olive oil, 1 clove garlic, 1 bay leaf, basil leaves, salt, pepper

If using fresh tomatoes, scald and peel. Place the tomatoes in a food mill over a bowl and grind into a purée. Chop the onion and cook in the olive oil until golden. Add the de-seeded and chopped red pepper, crushed garlic, bay leaf, basil, and puréed tomatoes, salt and pepper to the onion. Blend well. Simmer the mixture until it has reduced by one-half. Correct the seasoning. If the tomatoes are too acid, add a dash of sugar.

RICOTTA MOUSSE

Serves 6
4 cups Dolomites cow's milk (or fresh, whole milk), 1 vanilla bean, ½ lemon, 2 tbsps. pine nuts, 2 tbsps. raisins, ½ cup liquid honey

Heat the milk over low heat (158°F) with the vanilla bean and the lemon juice (or rennet). Allow the mixture to cool for 1 hour. Place a strainer over a bowl, line it with cheesecloth, and pour the thickened mixture into it. Allow the mixture to strain into the bowl until most of the whey has been drained off. Serve the mousse with the honey, pine nuts, and raisins (Corinth or Smyrna).

La Polenta,
Pietro Longhi,
Ca' Rezzonico.

VICENZA AND TREVISO

Vicenza and Treviso stand less than forty miles apart on a line that runs through the center of Venezia, down to Verona, below the foothills of the Dolomites. Vicenza, which joined the Venetian Republic in 1404, was once an ancient Roman city. Today a designated UNESCO World Heritage site, it owes its rank as a gem of the Renaissance to Andrea Palladio. The great architect designed some of the city's most remarkable monuments, after first saving from ruin a deteriorating Gothic building—the Palazzo della Ragione—by adding a supporting colonnade and a balustrade adorned with 23 statues. Four centuries later, this building still stands on the Piazza dei Signori, overlooked by the elegant Torre di Piazza dating from the twelfth century, dubbed the *Basilica Palladiana* in reference to its copper roof patinated by oxidation. Palladio also designed the Loggia del Capitaniato opposite, for the façade of which he used an astute combination of red brick and white stone. On the Contra Porti, a nearby street, the brilliant Paduan left his mark on three *palazzi*: the Palazzo Thiene, the Palazzo Porto Barbarano, and the Palazzo Iseppo da Porto. We are likewise indebted to him for the Palazzo Chiericati, the most original of his masterpieces, which now houses the Pinacoteca; he also designed the Teatro Olimpico, which was commissioned by the Olympic Academy. Palladio was not able to supervise construction work for the Teatro Olimpico, since he died at its outset. His son took

over and, in collaboration with Francesco Scamozzi, completed this stunning *trompe-l'œil* palace built on the ruins of an ancient *château*. Its interior projects the illusion of antiquity revisited, a stylistic staple during the Renaissance. Here, we have make-believe building materials (ordinary wood, plaster, and stucco imitating marble and stone), and—through the architectural structure rising at the rear of a stage—an illusion of distance, the structure in question being cleverly designed to afford a stunning vista culminating in a dream-like city behind a row of ornamental columns, pilasters, and statuary. Tiers of imitation marble benches (actually made of wood) rise around an amphitheater designed to resemble those of ancient Greece and Rome. The frescoed interiors of two smaller theaters (the odeon and antiodeon) on either side of the main building, used as lecture and concert halls, are less elaborate but just as elegant. The Olimpico's spacious courtyard-garden entrance is reached through an impressive stone gateway decorated with the Goethe *largo* shield.

The Teatro Olimpico was inaugurated on March 3rd, 1585. The play was Sophocles's *Œdipus Rex*, newly translated into the vernacular tongue that first developed in Tuscany and had only recently become the official literary language of Italy. The first members of the audience arrived at four o'clock in the afternoon for a performance that began at midnight and lasted until dawn. The setting was grandiose: magnificent sets, exquisite costumes, and exotic fragrances combined to ensure a glorious triumph, the theater's first. And its last, at least for centuries to come. The Olimpico's

STATUE OF ANDREA PALLADIO IN VICENZA, HIS HOME FOR MANY YEARS. HE DESIGNED NUMEROUS MAGNIFICENT MONUMENTS FOR THE CITY, INCLUDING THE "BASILICA," THE TEATRO OLIMPICO, AND THE VILLA ROTONDA.

THE RAKED BENCHES AND TROMPE-L'ŒIL DÉCOR OF THE TEATRO OLIMPICO, THE FIRST OPERA HOUSE, DESIGNED BY PALLADIO.

doors were closed by the Counter-Reformation, and they remained closed, curiously, until 1935. The nearby Church of Santa Corona was built to house what was believed to be a splinter of the cross on which Christ was crucified, and a thorn from the crown worn during the Crucifixion. The body of Luigi da Porto, the author from whom Shakespeare borrowed the story of Romeo and Juliet, lies in one of the church's chapels, and two major works of the Venetian Renaissance hang in the nave: Bellini's *Baptism of Christ* and Veronese's *Adoration of the Magi*.

Vincenzo Scamozzi, the Teatro Olimpico's brilliant set designer, also

THE SALVI GARDENS NEAR THE CENTER OF THE CITY, A FINE PLACE FOR A STROLL.

The Basilica
Santuario di Monte
Berico (above).

The people of
Vicenza can enjoy the
shade provided by
the arcades of the
"Basilica Palladiana"
(left).

A TYPICAL TREVISO
HOUSE, THE CASA
AFFRESCATA.

supervised completion of the Villa Rotonda begun fourteen years earlier. This villa is quintessentially Palladian: the work of a man who gave full rein to an imagination drawing on antique models, tactfully integrating into the local landscape a square structure surmounted by a dome and decorated on all four sides by porticos in the Roman-temple style. This flawless geometry makes the noble building—in which Joseph Losey filmed his *Don Giovanni*—a peerless example of Palladio's architectural ideals and genius.

Treviso, with fewer luxurious palaces than Vicenza, is less impressive. But the old town, lying between the Sile and Botteniga rivers and criss-crossed by canals, has its own special charm. Treviso was the native city of painter Paris Bordone (1500–1571) and was home for a time to Lorenzo Lotto (1480–1556), who left a number of frescos there. It does not have any exceptional monuments, but its narrow streets are appealing, and traces of old frescos can still be seen on the pretty houses lining them. The Piazza dei Signori has retained its medieval flavor, as have the Palazzo del Trecento (to which a few arcades were added in the sixteenth century) and the Loggia dei Cavalieri. The Via Calmaggiore leading to the cathedral has all the elegance of the Renaissance. It is a pleasure to stroll between its two rows of attractive shops on the way to the Casa da Noal (or Casa Tevigiana), a decorative-

THE PIAZZA DEI SIGNORI HAS BEEN A MEETING-PLACE FOR THE PEOPLE OF VICENZA EVER SINCE THE MIDDLE AGES.

making this altarpiece an exceptionally fine work of art. An incongruous juxta-position of ideas—one of the delights of travel—reminds us at this point that the eponymous company founded by Luciano Benetton, which has since become famous throughout the world for its vividly colo-red clothing, was founded here, at Treviso, in 1965. Benetton, a dynamic manager with a gift for public relations, also founded a decorative arts research institute, La Fabbrica, to encourage and support talented young designers.

Treviso (a small russet-leaved lettuce similar to chicory), although familiar out-side Italy, is far from the only agricultural resource in this region dominated by vineyards. The western Castellana plain is ideal for produce farming. Here we also find the birthplace—in Castelfranco Veneto, a small fortified town—of Giorgiono, who painted the noble Virgin on the altarpiece of the cathedral, and whose house is open to the public. The Villa Emo (with frescos by Gianbattista Zelotti) at Fanzolo, the Villa Lattès at Istrana, and a few other manors in the area are also open to the public during the summer months. In the north, climbing toward Belluno and the Dolomites, vineyards are omnipresent around Conegliano, also known for having

AN *ENOTECA*, OR WINE BAR, IN TREVISO. THE TOWN IS LESS THAN TWENTY MILES FROM THE "WHITE WINE ROUTE" RUNNING THROUGH THE *PROSECCO* VINEYARDS FROM CONEGLIANO TO VALDOBBIADENE.

THE CERAMIC ART TYPICAL OF BASSANO DEL GRAPPA.

arts museum; to the Luigi Bailo museum, which possesses some fine paintings (Bellini, Titian, Jacopo Bassano); and then to the fish market, *la pescheria*, held on an island in the Sile—a charming set-ting drawing pedestrians back to the Middle Ages. In churches dedicated to Saint Nicolas, Saint Francis, and Saint Catherine, visitors can admire the Gothic frescos of Tomaso da Modena, a precursor of the great Venetian school of art. Pordenone's *Adoration of the Magi* in the cathedral is admir-able for its daringly off-center composition, and Titian's *Annunciation* is a highly theatrical version of a scene we usually expect to be depicted with more tenderness and mystery. The Virgin's red robe and blue stole also contribute to produced Cima da Conegliano, an excellent painter who worked extensively in Venice and the surrounding region. The Strada del Vino Bianco (White Wine Route) leads to Valdobbiadene, a good place to stop and enjoy (in moderation!) a glass of *prosecco* or *cartizze*, a sparkling white wine. In the east, on the lagoon, Caorle is a fishing port and coastal resort. Its cathedral contains a Byzantine altarpiece—a *pala d'oro* similar to the one in Venice—of widespread fame, and the nearby town of Portogruaro has carefully preserved numerous relics of its glorious Roman past.

North of the main road, halfway between Vicenza and Treviso above the twin towns of Castelfranco and Citadella (the former square, flying the colors of Treviso; the latter round, flying those of Vicenza) the pretty town of Bassano del Grappa, its name taken from the mountain above it, nestles in the valley of the Brenta river, here spanned by a graceful covered wooden bridge. The town's name also evokes, of course, the famous liqueur found all over Italy and here represented by a museum and several excellent distilleries. The liqueur is *grappa*, a word derived from *graspa*, the lees-of-wine used in its distillation. To art lovers,

WINE BOTTLES AT THE AZIENDA AGRICOLA CA' LUGHETTA.

THESE GRAPES WILL BE MADE INTO WINE OR *GRAPPA*, THE BEST LIQUEUR IN ITALY.

THE CASTELFRANCO VENETO IS A FINE FORTIFIED VILLA ABOUT 12 MILES FROM TREVISO. GIORGIONE WAS BORN THERE IN 1478, AND THE LOCAL CATHEDRAL POSSESSES SIX OF HIS WORKS.

Bassano is the name of a painter: Jacopo da Ponte (1510–1592), who adopted the name of his native town (a pseudonym also used by his two painter sons, Leandro and Francesco). This luminous and resolutely bucolic artist is well represented here by 17 works displayed in the Museo Civico, which also holds a fine collection of Greek pottery. The Palazzo Sturm von Hirschfeld has assembled an array of Venetian majolica, most from the kilns of the two major factories once located in Bassano and Nove. A small town renowned its for ceramics since the twelfth century, nearby Nove also has a *palazzo* with an even larger collection. Standing on the point where plain

SIGN OVER THE TRATTORIA AL CASTELLETTO IN FOLLINA.

VENEZIA GRAPE VINES
GROW MUCH TALLER
THAN THOSE OF
BORDEAUX. THE GRAPE
PICKERS STAND WHILE
HARVESTING THE
GRAPES.

SIGN DIRECTING
TRAVELERS TO THE
WINE ROUTE.

THE CHURCH OF SAN
PIETRO DI FELETTO,
ITS SPIRE SEEMING TO
RISE DIRECTLY FROM
THE VINEYARDS.

A MEDIEVAL CASTLE
OVERLOOKS
CONEGLIANO,
BIRTHPLACE OF THE
GREAT PAINTER
CIMA DA CONEGLIANO
(1460–1518).

and mountains meet, Bassano is the proud center of an agricultural region that indeed has much to recommend it. Gastronomy comes naturally to the local populace, and a number of special events offer good reasons to visit during the autumn. This is the time when the grape harvest encourages the convivial sharing of local treasures. The Sant' Eusebio Grape Festival is just one of many opportunities to taste the region's wines. Neighboring villages also sponsor various festivals.

Trout and mushrooms are frequently featured on regional menus. In the spring, celery, beans, and asparagus have their hour of glory. Four miles away, the impressive fortified town of Marostica is famous for its monumental chess game, in which actors dressed in period costume take the place of the chessmen and make the moves on a vast chessboard.

Asolo, probably the loveliest village in Venezia, also stands at the foot of Mount Grappa, a little farther to the east. At the end of the sixteenth century, when Catherine Cornaro, the queen of Cyprus, was forced by the Venetians to yield her kingdom, she moved here with her court for a few years. A sweet exile indeed: the site is ravishing, and Asolo itself is a haven of grace. At the foot of the queen's

THE SCULPTOR CANOVA
IS BURIED IN THIS NEO-
CLASSIC TEMPLE
(ABOVE) BUILT IN
1830. THE HOUSE IN
WHICH HE WAS BORN
AND A MUSEUM
CONTAINING MODELS OF
HIS WORKS ARE BOTH
OPEN TO THE PUBLIC.

THE VILLA BARBARO,
BUILT BY PALLADIO, IS
LOCATED ABOUT 12
MILES FROM BASSANO
DEL GRAPPA. THE
SCULPTURES ON THE
VILLA'S EXTERIOR ARE
BY VERONESE (RIGHT).

THE VILLA CIPRIANI IN
ASOLO WAS BUILT IN
THE SIXTEENTH
CENTURY AND WAS
LATER CONVERTED INTO
A CHARMING HOTEL.

castle, the town's narrow winding streets evoke memories of two strong personalities, La Duse (the Italian Sarah Bernhardt, born in Asolo) and Robert Browning, one of whose works was a collection entitled *Asolando*. At Maser, six miles to the east, the Villa Barbaro is the happy result of a meeting between Palladio and Veronese. This is one of the finest and most impressive villas in Venezia, perfectly integrated into the landscape and extremely well preserved. Two large wings flank the protruding façade of the main building at right-angles. The courtyard at the rear leads to a very elegant pool. A little farther south, in Pasagno, sculptor Antonio Canova (1757–1822) is buried in the Tempio Canoviano, a temple for which he drew up the blueprints himself. The house where he was born and the Gypsoteca, in which are displayed plaster models of his works, are both open to the public. On the far side of Mount Grappa, higher up in the Dolomites, lies the plain of the Seven Towns, on the borderline between Trentino and Upper Adige. Here we are high in the mountains, in a region notable for the fact that in 1310, seven villages—whose inhabitants had come from Bavaria two years earlier—formed a federation that retained its distinctive character over the intervening centuries, even preserving a little of its ancient culture. The largest of the seven, Asiago, is now a well known winter and summer resort.

TONI SAUTÉS
SPRING
VEGETABLES IN
THE KITCHEN OF
HIS RESTAURANT,
L'OSTERIA.

BASSANO ASPARAGUS WITH SHIRRED EGGS

Serves 6

2 bunches white Bassano
asparagus (similar to the variety
found in France),
6 eggs, olive oil,
balsamic vinegar,
salt, pepper

Carefully peel the asparagus. Boil them in salted water or steam them for 10 to 20 minutes, depending on their size. Drain, transfer to a plate, and cover with a cloth to keep warm. Prepare shirred eggs: immerse the eggs in boiling water and cook them for 4 to 5 minutes. Shell the eggs and mash them with a fork. Season them with salt, pepper, olive oil, and balsamic vinegar. Remove the cloth from the plate, arrange the asparagus around the sides, and place the shirred-egg mixture in the center. An alternative way to serve the asparagus is with a soft-boiled egg in the center, for dipping. This recipe can also be made with green baby asparagus. In this case, cook them for 5 minutes, then immerse them in a bowl of ice water (as for green beans) for a few moments, and drain them before serving. The ice water keeps the asparagus firm and green. For a sophisticated touch, instead of salting the egg, garnish it with a little Beluga caviar.

GRILLED RADICCHIO OR RADICCHIO FRITTERS

Serves 6

6 heads radicchio lettuce,
1 cup flour, 1 egg,
1 cup breadcrumbs,
oil for deep-fat frying, salt

This lettuce, a rarity outside of Treviso, owes the secret of its flavor to the purity of the water in which it grows—which also explains the white color at the base of the leaves.

Remove the outer leaves from the radicchio. Cut the hearts in half lengthwise, rinse them thoroughly, and wipe them dry. Dredge the hearts in the flour, shaking well to remove the excess. Beat the egg. Dip the dredged hearts in the beaten egg, then roll them in the breadcrumbs. Deep-fry them in hot oil, and drain them on absorbent paper. The radicchio may also be dipped in olive oil and grilled. Season with salt, and serve.

RISOTTO WITH TREVISO RADICCHIO

Serves 4

4 heads Treviso radicchio lettuce,
½ cup olive oil, 1 onion, 6 tbsps.
butter, 1½ cups *Arborio Super
Fino* rice, ½ cup white wine,
4 cups hot chicken or vegetable
broth, salt, pepper,
4 tbsps. Parmesan cheese

Rinse the radicchio thoroughly, wipe dry. Cut the heads in four lengthwise and then in two crosswise. Sauté the lettuce briefly over high heat in a little olive oil (to remove the bitter flavor). Set aside. Chop the onion. Heat the remaining olive oil and a little of the butter in a casserole over medium heat. Add the onions and cook for about 10 minutes, until soft but not golden. Add the rice and the hot broth (see p. 124 for recipe). Season with salt and pepper. Add the wine, stirring until it evaporates. Cover, and simmer for 15 minutes, adding broth if necessary to prevent sticking. Add the radicchio and continue simmering until the rice is done. Add the Parmesan cheese and the remaining butter, stirring vigorously to obtain the creamy blend known as *mantecare.*

TREVISO-STYLE TRIPE

Serves 6

2½ lbs. boiled calves tripe,
1 onion, 2 tbsps. olive oil,
4 tbsps. diced bacon, a few sprigs
of rosemary, 2 cups hot beef
broth, 12 thin slices bread,
7 tbsps. grated Parmesan cheese,
black pepper from the mill

Order cleaned, pre-cooked tripe from your butcher. Cut the tripe into narrow strips. Slice the onion. Heat the olive oil over a medium heat in a skillet. Add the sliced onion and diced bacon, cook until golden. Add the tripe and rosemary, stirring and simmering briefly. Add the hot beef broth. Simmer for 2 hours (for raw tripe, simmer for at least 3 hours). Toast the bread. Warm 6 dinner plates and place 2 slices of toast in each one. Pour the tripe and broth over the toast. Sprinkle with a generous amount of grated Parmesan cheese. Season to taste with freshly ground pepper. Serve.

VINCENTINA-STYLE STOCKFISH

Serves 6

2 pounds stockfish (unsalted, air-cured cod), 3 tbsps. flour,
3 onions, 2 cloves garlic, 1 cup olive oil, 1 bunch parsley, 3 anchovies, 2 tbsps. grated Parmesan cheese, 1 cup white wine, 2 cups milk, salt, pepper

Soak the fish overnight in cold water to cover. Drain and wipe dry. Skin the fish and remove the central bone. Cut into large pieces and dredge with flour. Preheat oven to 250°F. Slice the onion, chop the garlic and the parsley. Heat the olive oil in a skillet over medium heat. Add the onion and garlic. When they begin to color, add the parsley and the anchovies. Place the dredged pieces of fish in an ovenproof earthenware

pan just large enough to hold them in a single layer. Add the onion, garlic, parsley, anchovies, and Parmesan cheese. Season with salt and pepper. Add the white wine. Scald the milk and pour it into the pan over the other ingredients. Cover with a lid or aluminum foil. Bake for 4 to 5 hours. Serve hot, with polenta.

PIGEON SOUP

Serves 6

3 young pigeons, 1 large onion,
2 celery stalks, 2 carrots, ¼ cup olive oil, ½ cup dry white wine,
8 cups hot chicken broth, salt, pepper, 1 lb. stale bread (sliced), 8 tbsps. butter, 7 tbsps. grated Parmesan cheese

This Italian-style soup can be served as a main dish. It requires lengthy preparation and improves in flavor when served the day after it is made.

Preheat oven to 350°F. If you do not prepare your own pigeons, order plucked and cleaned birds from the butcher. Cut off and discard the heads and feet, set the livers aside. Cut each bird in two lengthwise, and again in two crosswise. Chop the onion, celery, and carrots. Heat the olive oil in a large casserole over high heat. Sauté the vegetables until golden, remove with a skimmer and set aside. Add the cut-up pigeons to the pan and brown on all sides. Return the vegetables to the casserole and add the white wine, simmering until the wine evaporates. Add half of the hot broth. Season to taste, cover, and simmer 25 minutes. Add the livers and simmer 5 minutes longer.

Remove the livers and cut-up pigeons from the broth. Discard the bones, cut the livers and pieces of pigeon in half. Meanwhile, pour the rest of the hot broth into the casserole with the vegetables. Add the juice from the cut-up pigeons and simmer for approximately 10 minutes. Sauté the bread slices in the butter. Remove the vegetables from the broth, put through a food mill, and return to broth. Stir to blend. Place a layer of bread slices on the bottom of a clean ovenproof casserole. Cover with a layer of pigeon sections and livers. Repeat, ending with a layer of bread. Add the broth. Top with grated Parmesan cheese. Bake for 2½ hours.

TIRAMISÙ

Serves 6

2 lbs. Mascarpone cream cheese (available in specialty food shops), 8 egg yolks, 11 tbsps. sugar, 1 cup Marsala, 2 cups strong hot espresso-type coffee, 30 lady fingers, 2 tbsps. powdered cocoa

Make a zabaglione (for recipe, see p. 54) with the egg yolks, 8 tbsps. of the sugar, and the Marsala. Add the Mascarpone to the zabaglione and whip to blend thoroughly. Add the remaining 3 tbsps. sugar to the hot coffee. Cool the coffee to lukewarm and add the lady fingers (if the coffee is too hot they will crumble, if too cold they will not absorb the liquid). Arrange the soaked lady fingers side-by-side in a serving dish. Cover with the zabaglione mixture. If desired, the lady fingers can be arranged in two layers, ending with a second layer of zabaglione. Allow to rest for 2 hours in a cool spot or the refrigerator, but do not prepare the day before. Dust the top of the Tiramisù with cocoa sifted through a strainer. Serve.

CAFFÉ ILLY, PROCESSED IN TRIESTE, IS THE VENETIAN COFFEE *PAR EXCELLENCE*. MOST ITALIAN COFFEE COMES FROM THE REGION AROUND NAPLES.

MASCARPONE IS A HIGH-FAT CHEESE MADE FROM COW'S MILK. IT IS ESPECIALLY GOOD WITH PASTA.

In springtime, the markets of Venezia display all sorts of crisp, delicious greens. These make delectable salads when mixed with a little dill, basil, or wild fennel and seasoned with balsamic vinegar, olive oil, salt, and pepper.

CHAPTER VI
PADUA AND THE SOUTH

In fine weather you can embark on the *Burchiello* for a trip up the Brenta canal, reaching Padua in a little less than eight hours. Named after the boat that plied the same waterway in former times, the *Burchiello* glides smoothly between the Palladian villas built along the banks of the canal. In the sixteenth century, wealthy Venetians—in search of fresh sources of revenue at a time of diminishing maritime trade—were no longer satisfied with the absentee cultivation of estates gradually being turned over to corn. They developed a taste for country living, and commissioned summer residences from the best architects. Andrea Palladio (1508–1580) was the undisputed master of this rural architecture reflecting the renewed interest in nature characteristic of the Renaissance. Obsessed by a highly mathematical sense of harmony, this son of a Paduan miller cultivated an idealist conception of beauty based on pure humanism enhanced by overt theatricality. And yet, Palladio consistently respected the function of the

structures he designed, lavishing as much care on utilitarian outbuildings as on the manor-houses themselves. He built at least twenty villas scattered throughout Venezia. The one closest to Venice, practically on the banks of the lagoon, is an imposing residence of extraordinarily harmonious proportions providing an appropriate setting for the leisured life. On its southern side, light floods in through a wide bay window, while the main façade faces the canal with a colonnade, an ornamental entranceway, and a double staircase for welcoming visitors arriving by boat. The frescos decorating the interior walls are by Gianbattista Zelotti, a once famous artist who worked extensively in the region.

A short cruise on the *Burchiello* also provides an opportunity to visit two other villas, the Villa Pisani in Stra, and the Villa Widman-Foscari in Mira. The former was commissioned by the doge Alvise Pisani from architect Francesco Maria Preti, and its 114 reception rooms project an astounding degree of megalomania—

PALLADIO RAISED THE GROUND FLOOR OF "LA MALCONTENTA" (LEFT AND ABOVE) AS A PRECAUTION AGAINST FLOODING.

THE VILLA FOSCARI IS KNOWN FAMILIARLY AS "LA MALCONTENTA." PALLADIO BUILT IT ON THE BANKS OF THE BRENTA BETWEEN PADUA AND THE LAGOON, NOT FAR FROM VENICE (LEFT).

THE VILLA BARBARO IN MASER, BUILT IN 1555 (PREVIOUS DOUBLE PAGE).

FRESCO BY VERONESE AT THE VILLA BARBARO, ABOUT SIX MILES TO THE EAST OF ASOLO.

with villas, many of them as yet unrestored (for this is an enormous task; Venezia boasts over 400 of these villas, all considered a regional artistic heritage of the highest order), exuding a somewhat melancholy grandeur but coexisting peaceably with less attractive neighbors. At Piazzola sul Brenta, for example, the beauty of the Villa Contarini is marred by the presence of an adjacent factory. Venice's social elite became accustomed to abandoning the city's canals during the summer months for the pleasures of the Brenta. The *Burchiello* was the perfect instrument of this novel Venetian fad, an aristocratic omnibus for summer pleasure-seekers, a

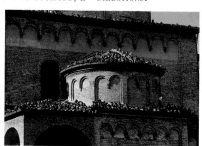

confirmed when it was chosen by Hitler and Mussolini as the setting for their meeting in 1934. Tiepolo painted a huge fresco on the ballroom ceiling, and the park—with its open-air pavilions, hot-houses, orangery, maze, and belvedere—is one of the most beautiful anywhere in Italy. The rococo décor of the Villa Widman-Foscari is less grandiose, but has a more intimate charm.

Travelers on the road running alongside the Brenta will appreciate the charm of a bank bordered with willows, even though the landscape is marred by the industrial development of Porto Marghera, the somewhat shameful annex of a Venice reluctant to admit the economic imperatives of modern times. The land is dotted

sumptuous yet carefree vehicle of fashion. The serious business of agriculture was forgotten during the eighteenth century, as Venetian society—now in decline and no longer able to identify with the proud and ancient republic of which it had once been part—sought headier pleasures in country palaces fully as magnificent as those in the city, and in parks where orchestras and fireworks led a brilliant dance that fanned the guttering flame of a Most Serene city growing uncertain of its serenity. Even now, on a Sunday in September

THE PRATO DELLA
VALLE (MEADOW IN THE
VALLEY) AT PADUA HAS
SERVED SINCE ROMAN
TIMES AS THE SITE OF
POPULAR FESTIVALS.
IMPROVEMENTS WERE
MADE TO IT DURING THE
EIGHTEENTH CENTURY.

designated for the annual commemoration of this happier time, dozens of boats filled with happy pleasure-seekers repeat the traditional excursion up the Brenta.

Padua (22 miles away from Venice) is a bustling, sprawling city with no obvious attraction for tourists. However, in the center of the city visitors can enjoy the impression of having stepped into a painting by Giorgio de Chirico, especially on holidays or at quiet times of day (dawn is best, when the light encourages reverie). Squares, streets, and arcades seem to recede into infinity from the hub of the city, a monument that is one of Venezia's most imposing (and most elegant): the Palazzo della Ragione. This building is the town hall, its front and rear façades each overlooking a square—the Piazza delle Erbe (vegetables) on one side, and the Piazza della Fruta

(fruits) on the other. In these two squares, the city's open market is held. This municipal building was constructed in the early twelfth century, and has a single room (256 feet long, 88 feet wide, 85 feet high) on its upper floor. The original vaulting, painted with astral symbols by Giotto, was destroyed by fire in 1420. After the fire, Nicola Miretto was commissioned to decorate the room with 333 frescos, and these have survived. The Pedrocchi café, a neoclassic folly built during the first half of the nineteenth century, is just a few steps away. The Pedrocchi is Padua's fashionable meeting-place. It also has

THE MARRIAGE FEAST
OF ALEXANDER AND
ROXANNE, BY
GIAMBATTISTA CROSATO
(1686–1758). FRESCO
IN THE VILLA
MARCELLO, PADUA.

a historic past as the nerve-center of opposition to the 1848 Austrian occupation. For many years it remained open day and night, and it still has a room where customers can linger to read, chat, or play cards, under no obligation to order. Recent renovations have destroyed much of its original charm, a mishap for which Saint Anthony (of Padua, naturally) is blamed. Local wags claim the saint was jealous of this pagan establishment's competition with the great church in which his mortal remains are laid to rest. Saint Anthony (1195–1231), originally from Portugal, preached against the rich and their insensitivity to the misery of the less fortunate. Today he would no doubt view with considerable irony the commerce flourishing around his sanctuary, and the

fleets of profitable tourist buses filled with pilgrims to his shrine. The Basilica of Saint Anthony (Il Santo) is a vast Romanesque edifice visibly marked by Byzantine influences (in its eight domes), balanced, on its façade, with Gothic touches. Although it is impressive, its size and over-elaborate decoration lend it a kitsch tone that inspires little emotion in visitors disinclined to worship the saint of lost objects. It was built to hold the body of a saint confidently expected to perform miracles after his death. When Saint Anthony's body was brought to the basilica for burial, the casket was opened and the saint's tongue,

jawbone, and fore-arm removed to serve as relics for veneration by the faithful. It is said that the tongue remained in a remarkable state of preservation for forty years afterwards and even, according to all reports, moved with lifelike flexibility. The high altar is adorned with a fine group of Donatello bronzes. The Saint Anthony chapel, which houses the holy burial site, features some interesting marble bas-reliefs from the hands of various Renaissance artists. Visitors touring this gloomy mausoleum might be tempted, afterwards, to sample the more earthly delights of a large brioche called *Dolce Santantonio* sold in the pastry shop out front. For those not who are not particular followers of

Saint Anthony, the Scrovegni chapel, decorated by Giotto (1267–1327), offers a more moving sight. The elder Scrovegni was a usurer, and his son commissioned the chapel in order to preserve him from eternal damnation. The building's sole merit resides in its function as a backdrop for one of the greatest treasures of Italian art: a cycle of 38 frescos executed by the admirable Giotto, who combined freshness and modesty with an original artistic style and novel experiments in perspective technique. Giotto devoted six years of his life to the work, the greater part of which recounts the life of Christ. The blue sky replacing the traditional Byzantine gold background unifies the whole, while imbuing it with a soft glow symbolic of a more human and more introspective spirituality. Giotto also executed original frescos for the Grand Council room of the Palazzo della Ragione, but they were destroyed by fire early in the fifteenth century. Giotto was not Paduan himself, but his fellow artist Andrea Mantegna (1431–1506) was. Unfortunately, however, few of the emotionally intense works by this greatest of all Padua's artists can be seen in his native city. There are no Mantegnas in the fine collection at the Museo Civico Eremitani, notable for a *Crucifixion* by Giotto and Veronese's *The Martyrdom of Saint Justine*. The Mantegna painting displayed

THE CHIOGGIA MARKET IS RENOWNED FOR ITS PICTURESQUE CHARM AND THE QUALITY OF ITS VEGETABLES AND FISH.

at the Eremitani Church next to the museum is a youthful work. Although only twenty-three years old when he painted the frescos in the Ovetari chapel (reputedly endowing the martyred Saint Christopher with his own features), he already exhibited consummate artistic authority. Padua is also home to a major university, founded in 1221 and known familiarly as "*Il Bo*" (the ox) after a tavern that once stood nearby. Despite its nickname, this institution is an eminently serious one: it was a center of intellectual ferment during the Renaissance (attracting Dante, Petrarch, and Galileo—who taught there for a dozen years or so) and has since been a driving

force in the advancement of the sciences, particularly medicine. This explains why Padua possesses the oldest botanical garden in Europe. Originally intended for the cultivation of medicinal plants, it also served as a home for Italy's first lilacs and sunflowers. Today it is still a superb, living museum of botanical specimens.

Venezia extends south of Padua to the Po valley, beyond which lies Emilia-Romagna. To the west are the nearby Euganian Hills, a regional park made up of extinct volcanoes forming a highly intriguing landscape despite their modest altitude (2,000 feet at most). The local vineyards produce a pleasant, fruity wine: the perfect accompaniment for pigeons grilled with pepper and juniper berries, Po river chicken, rice with peas, and pasta with haricot beans—all Paduan specialties. Dotted here and there are mineral springs already reputed in Roman times for their effectiveness against rheumatism. Abano Terme, only 5 miles from Padua, is still an active spa famous for its mud baths. Here, seemingly a thousand leagues from big-city industrial Venezia, travelers can forget the crowds and discover the bucolic Italy celebrated by Petrarch (1303–1374), one of the first major Italian poets to abandon Latin for the Italian vernacular. Petrarch spent the last four years of his life in a medieval village today called Arqua Petrarca. The poet's house, vigilantly guarded by his stuffed cat, is open to the public, and his body rests in the Church of Santa Maria. At nearby Monselice, a peaceful nature reserve offers a protected environment to endangered species of birds of prey that are threatened with extinction. Another pleasant stop among these charming hills is Valsanzibio, where the Villa Barbarigo rises like a tiny pink gem at the center of a superb garden filled with fountains. A visit should also be made to the Benedictine monks of Praglia abbey, who grow their own vegetables and restore rare books in the most delightful of natural settings. An impressive sight is the imposing sixteenth-century Cataio Castle, its turrets and drawbridge built in a style contrasting dramatically with Palladio's contemporary designs.

THE BRENTA RIVER FLOWS FROM THE DOLOMITES, THROUGH BASSANO DEL GRAPPA AND PADUA, TO VENICE.

THE ASTRONOMICAL OBSERVATORY AT PADUA.

Continuing our trip away from Padua to the other side of the hills, we reach Este, and the ruined Castello dei Carraresi looming above it—which inspired two of England's greatest romantic poets, Byron and Shelley, to raptures of lyricism. This was the first area in Venezia to be settled, and vestiges of the civilization it produced in 1000 B.C. are displayed in the Museo Nazionale Atestino. In the eighteenth century, Este also became a center for the ceramic arts. White-enameled statuettes and pottery glazed with "Este blue" have spread the fame of these local artifacts, highly prized by the Venetians.

THE RAMPARTS OF CITTADELLA, BUILT IN THE THIRTEENTH CENTURY, ARE STILL INTACT.

South of Este we soon reach the Adige river, which flows from Verona into the Adriatic just above Chioggia—a pretty port on the lagoon where a fish and sea-food market on the Canale della Vena offers a lively spectacle. Here, only sixteen miles from Venice, is the perfect place for sampling the region's crabs and cuttlefish. A pleasant destination for a summer excursion is the beach at Sottomarina, where the Church of San Domenico displays Carpaccio's last work, a painting of Saint Paul. It is here that the Polesine begins—the flat and misty landscape of the Po delta. The Po is a temperamental river, but its violent flooding has improved the fertility of the land around it. Rice, corn, and beets are now grown in the area dominated by the town of Rovigo (with a lovely octagonal church, a Rotunda, and a not insignificant art museum containing two works by Bellini). A large protected natural park shelters a vast number of species of birds—including herons, curlews, egrets, and bitterns—and two holiday resorts, Rosolina Mare and Isola Albarella, are recommended as good bases from which to set out on botanical or bird-watching excursions. Adria is now an inland town, but was once proudly situated on the coast of the Adriatic to which it gave its name. The sea receded, leaving the town with only a memory of its original status.

CERAMICS PRODUCED BY MARCO PIZZATO IN ESTE.

THE CORN FROM WHICH POLENTA IS MADE.

THE TRATTORIA AL
MOLIN, IN VECIO
CALDOGNO.

THE PO DELTA. THE PO
RIVER HAS FINALLY BEEN
BROUGHT UNDER
CONTROL, AND ITS ONCE
EXTREMELY UNSTABLE
DELTA IS NOW A NATURE
RESERVATION.

THERE ARE MANY
BRANDS OF ITALIAN
RICE. *ACQUARELLO*,
ALSO KNOWN AS *RISO
D'AUTORE*, IS SUITABLE
FOR ALL TYPES OF
RISOTTO. OTHER GOOD
BRANDS INCLUDE *GALLO*,
SCOTTI, AND *RISO
ARBORIO*.

BASIC RISOTTO

Serves 4

3 tbsps. olive oil, 1 mild onion,
1½ cups round rice, ½ cup wine,
4–6 cups hot broth, 6 tbsps.
grated Parmesan cheese,
2 tbsps. butter

Risotto is traditionally stirred constantly during cooking. Toni has developed an easier method, but you will still need a vigilant eye. Plan on 4–6 cups of broth when making a risotto, and be sure it is boiling hot when you add it to the rice. Most risottos are cooked before adding the final garnish (mushrooms, clams, etc.), but the juices from the separate preparation of the garnish should be added to the rice with the broth. You will have three pots on your stove: the casserole for the rice, the pot of hot broth, and a pan for cooking the garnish.

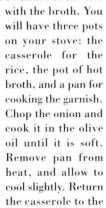

Chop the onion and cook it in the olive oil until it is soft. Remove pan from heat, and allow to cool slightly. Return the casserole to the heat, add the rice, and cook for 2 minutes, stirring continuously. Add the wine. When it has evaporated, add the hot broth and the juices from the preparation of the garnish. The liquid should rise to one inch above the surface of the rice. Cover, reduce the heat, and simmer the rice for about 15 minutes, checking often to see there is enough liquid to

prevent the rice from sticking. Just before the rice is done, add the prepared garnish. If the rice contains too much liquid, raise the heat under the casserole and boil, stirring, until all the broth has been absorbed by the rice. Add the grated Parmesan cheese and a knob of butter. Stir the mixture vigorously for 2 minutes over low heat. The final stirring breaks down the starch, giving the risotto a creamy consistency.

RISOTTO WITH PEAS

Serves 4

3 tbsps. olive oil, 4 tbsps. butter, 1 onion, 1 lb. peas, 1 bunch parsley, 1½ cups round rice, 4 cups vegetable broth, 6 tbsps. grated Parmesan cheese, salt

Shell the peas, peel and slice the onion, chop the parsley. Heat the olive oil and 3 tbsps. of the butter in a heavy casserole over medium heat. Add the onion and cook until soft but not colored. Add the peas, parsley, and 6 tbsps. of broth. Simmer for 15 minutes. Remove the peas with a skimmer and set aside. Add the rice and remaining broth, following the basic risotto recipe (above). Simmer, covered, until all the broth has been absorbed. Season to taste with salt. A few

minutes before the rice is done, return the cooked peas to the casserole. Adjust the seasoning. Add the grated Parmesan cheese and a knob (1 tbsp.) of butter.

SPRING RISOTTO

Serves 4

4 dwarf Italian artichokes (*castraure*), 1 carrot, 1 stalk celery, 1 tomato, 1 onion, ¾ lb. baby green asparagus, ¾ lb. fresh green peas, 1 small zucchini, 3 tbsps. olive oil, 4 tbsps. butter, 1½ cups round rice, ½ cup white wine, 4 cups vegetable broth, basil leaves, parsley (or chopped spinach), 4 tbsps. + 1 cup grated Parmesan cheese, salt, pepper

Prepare and sauté the artichokes (see p. 76). Chop the carrot and celery. Scald and peel the tomato, slice the onion. Cut the tips off the asparagus and set aside, slice the stems. Slice the zucchini and set aside. Shell the peas. Place the olive oil and 3 tbsps. butter in a heavy casserole over a medium heat. Add the peas and 6 tbsps. of the broth. Reduce heat and simmer 15 minutes. Remove the peas with a skimmer and set aside. Add the onions to the casserole, cooking until transparent. Add a little oil and butter to the casserole if needed, and then add the asparagus stems, carrot, celery, and tomato. Sauté briefly over low heat. Add the rice, white wine, and vegetable broth. Stir. Cover the casserole, and simmer 10 minutes. Add the zucchini, asparagus tips, peas,

TO CHECK PEAS FOR FRESHNESS, FIRST REMOVE THE PODS. THE PEAS INSIDE SHOULD BE REGULAR IN SHAPE, SMOOTH, UNDAMAGED, SMALL, AND SLIGHTLY SWEET IN FLAVOR—AS THEY ARE IN THE GARDEN.

artichokes, basil, and parsley. Cover and simmer for 5 more minutes. Add more broth if necessary. Season, dot with butter, sprinkle with Parmesan cheese and blend.

PUMPKIN RISOTTO

Serves 4

1 lb. pumpkin or Chioggia squash, 1½ cups round *Vialone Nano* rice, 4 cups vegetable or chicken broth, 1 tbsp. olive oil, 3 tbsps. butter, 1 onion, 1 bunch parsley, 1 cup grated Parmesan cheese, salt, pepper

Peel the pumpkin and remove the seeds. Chop into large pieces and then grate coarsely. Chop the onion and parsley. Place the olive oil and 2 tbsps. of the butter in a heavy casserole over medium heat. Add the chopped onion and cook until soft but not colored. Add the pumpkin, salt, and pepper. Cook, stirring, until reduced to a purée. Add the rice and stir. Heat the broth and add. Simmer, stirring occasionally, until the broth has been absorbed by the rice. Add the chopped parsley, salt and pepper to taste, and the remaining butter. Sprinkle some Parmesan cheese on top, and stir over a low heat until a creamy blend is obtained. Serve at once with a bowl of grated Parmesan cheese.

FIGS IN RED WINE

Serves 6
12 fresh figs,
1½ cups red wine,
3 tbsps. granulated sugar,
¼ lb. raspberries

Wash the figs, cut off their stems, and arrange in a shallow ovenproof pan, packing them closely, in a single layer. Add the wine, sugar, and raspberries. Place the pan in the preheated (425°F) oven and bake for

5 to 10 minutes, until the figs are soft. Transfer the figs to a serving dish, using a skimmer. Crush the raspberries in the pan juices, and reduce over low heat until syrupy. Strain onto the figs. Cool. Serve lukewarm or cold.

VEGETABLE BROTH

For use in risottos, soups, etc.
2 carrots, 2 stalks celery, 2 onions, 4 cloves, 1 bunch asparagus, 1 tomato, 2 sprigs parsley, 2 sprigs thyme, 1 bay leaf, 1 bunch basil, 8 cups water

Stud each onion with 2 cloves, and discard the tips from the asparagus. Place all the ingredients in water, and simmer for 20 minutes, skimming frequently during the cooking. Strain.

PEARS IN WHITE WINE

Serves 6
6 pears, 2 cups water, 1 cup white wine, 1 cup sugar or 4 tbsps. honey, peel of 2 lemons, 1 tsp. cinnamon

Put the sugar (or honey), water, wine, lemon peel, and cinnamon in a large pot and bring to the boil. Reduce the heat to low, cover, and simmer for about 10 minutes. Peel the pears, leaving them whole. Do not remove the stems. Add the pears to the pot. Bring to a boil. Lower the heat, cover, and simmer until the pears are soft but still hold their shape (about 15 minutes). Allow the pears to cool in the cooking liquid. Transfer to a serving dish and pour the cooking liquid over the pears. Sprinkle with cinnamon, and chill.

TAGLIATELLE WITH CHICKEN LIVERS

Serves 6
2 tbsps. olive oil, 1 lb. cleaned chicken livers, ½ cup Marsala, 1½ cups hot beef broth, 4 tbsps. butter, 1 tbsp. flour, 2 tbsps. fresh thyme, salt, pepper from the mill, 1½ lbs. Tagliatelle noodles

Split the chicken livers in half. Heat the olive oil over a high heat in a large skillet. Add the chicken livers and sauté them for 3 to 4 minutes on each side, stirring them vigorously. The livers are cooked when they begin to stick to the skillet. Add the Marsala to the skillet and set the liquid alight, using a match. Shake the skillet until the flames are extinguished. Remove the livers with a skimmer and set them aside. Add the beef broth to the skillet and scrape up the pan juices. Melt the butter in a pot, add the flour and cook for 1 to 2 minutes, stirring until smooth. Add the hot juices from the skillet, and the thyme. Whisk to obtain a smooth sauce. Simmer for 5 minutes, whisking occasionally. Season the sauce to taste with salt and pepper. Slice the chicken livers into narrow strips and add them to the sauce. Meanwhile, cook the noodles in a large pot of boiling water. When they are ready, drain and transfer them to a warm serving dish. Reheat the sauce and pour it over the noodles. Serve.

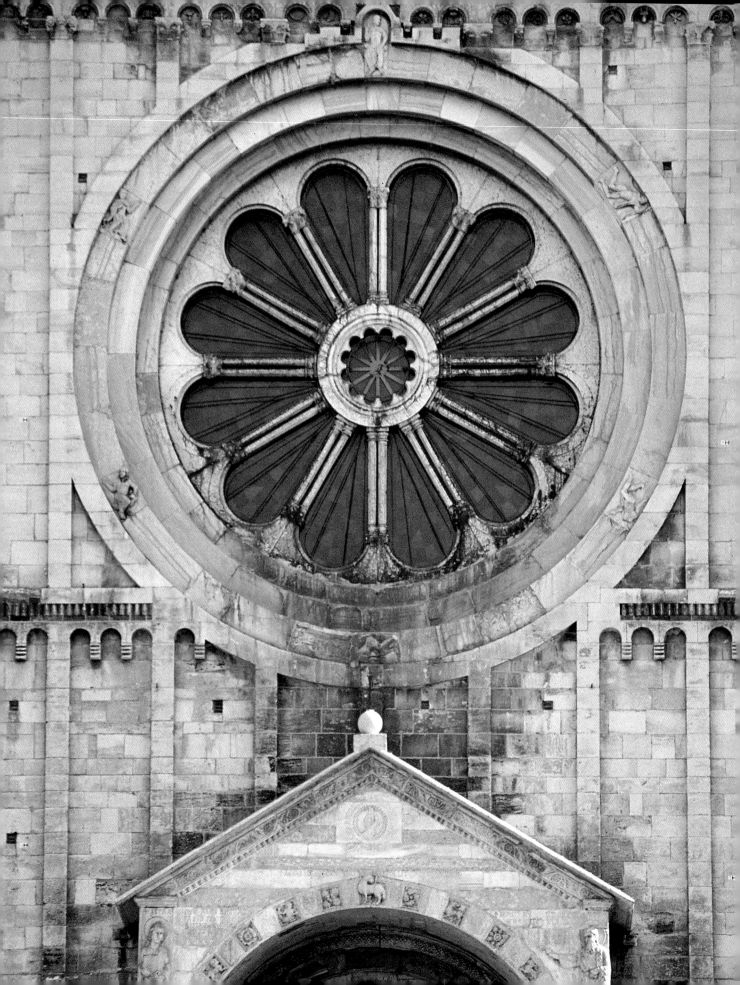

VERONA
AND LAKE GARDA

THE CHURCH OF SAN
ZENO MAGGIORE IS A
MASTERPIECE OF
ITALIAN ROMANESQUE
ART. ESPECIALLY
NOTABLE IS ITS FINE
MANTEGNA TRIPTYCH.

JULIET'S HOUSE AND
THE BALCONY UNDER
WHICH HER BETROTHED
ROMEO ONCE STOOD.
A VERY POPULAR
TOURIST ATTRACTION.

THE SAN ZENO
CLOISTERS.

Verona's two spiritual patrons are William Shakespeare and Saint Zeno. We know little about Saint Zeno except that he came from Africa, was named after a Greek philosopher obsessed with paradoxes, and had a sunny disposition. As the exception among so many dour saints, this was a virtue deserving special honor for the fourth-century bishop. Verona obliged, placing the city under his eternal guardianship and offering him its finest church—much finer than its banal cathedral. As for William Shakespeare, there are doubts in some quarters that he actually existed. But no one doubts that his Romeo and Juliet are an integral part of Verona's history! The Montagues and the Capulets were indeed lords of the city, and it is intriguing to imagine that the story of Romeo and Juliet (which Shakespeare borrowed from Luigi da Porto) really did take place in western Venezia. Thanks to those two famous star-crossed lovers, Verona is one of the world capitals of romance. To Venice belong the happy-go-lucky exploits of Casanova; but to Verona, the blood, tears, and tragedy of Romeo and Juliet. In the realm of music, which prefers emotions on an operatic scale, Shakespeare's successor was Verdi; in the paradise of tragic lovers, Aida and Juliet are equals. Juliet's house and grave are in Verona, and every summer the city opens its doors to music.

Verona, like Venice, is a city to fall in love with. It is not one of those beautiful cities you can skim as you would a book of art history or a glossy magazine, wandering from church to museum, or from luxury shop to fine restaurant. Like Venice, Verona is a city that inspires love rather than analysis, that opens itself to those who are prepared to open themselves to it.

Set in the Adige valley at the junction of the roads leading from Munich and Innsbruck to Florence and Rome, and from Basel and Zurich to Venice via Milan, Verona occupies a strategic spot

GIUSEPPE VERDI,
WHOSE OPERAS ARE
STILL A STAPLE ON
PROGRAMS AT THE
VERONA ARENA.

THE PARK AT THE
PALAZZO GIUSTI IS A
GEM OF THE ITALIAN
RENAISSANCE. GOETHE
LIKED TO STROLL HERE,
AND IT IS A FAVORITE
PICNIC SPOT FOR THE
CITIZENS OF VERONA
(PREVIOUS DOUBLE
PAGE).

in the heart of Venezia. It is therefore not surprising that the Romans made it into a major urban center at an early stage in their history. Nor is it surprising that the Germanic Holy Roman Empire later built a fortress there; and that in the nineteenth century it became an important garrison under the Austrian occupation. But geography does not explain everything, and Verona has charms other than its value to military strategists. The Valpolicella valley was an extremely pleasant spot before it became over-industrialized, and nearby Lake Garda has in every era (starting with the Romans, who appreciated wine and the good life) attracted more peaceable travelers.

Pink marble was used to build the medieval palaces of Verona at a time when the Scaligers were lords of the city. These men welcomed Dante to their city when the poet was in exile from Florence (a statue of him stands in the Piazza dei Signori). Above the city they erected the imposing Castelvecchio. This brick castle, serving as both a fortress and a palace, was built at the end of the fourteenth century and was converted into a museum in the middle of the twentieth century by the architect Carlo Scarpa. He completely transformed it by adding footbridges, corridors, and balconies—new solutions for the creation of an inviting museum interior. Present-day visitors to this museum's outstanding collection can appreciate the extent to which the art of Verona was influenced by the Germanic

SAN FERMO MAGGIORE
AND SAN GIORGIO IN
BRAIDA, TWO VERONA
CHURCHES ON THE
BANKS OF THE ADIGE.

countries to the north, before it achieved its own version of the Venetian style with artists such as Francesco Morone (1471–1529) and Liberale da Verona (1445–1529). The museum's walls also display works by Bellini, Veronese, and Tintoretto. In the courtyard there is a statue of Campogrande I sitting astride his horse, but it is the animal, rather than the rider, which commands admiration: it seems to have been modeled from life. The city, which lies in a bend of the Adige river, can be admired in its entirety from the road that encircles it. The Ponte Scaligero, once on the main road into the Tyrol, was destroyed during the Second World War and subsequently rebuilt

exactly as before. But now we are eager to explore the streets of the city itself, starting with the Corso Cavour; the Arco dei Gavi, triumphal souvenir of the Romans; the Romanesque Church of San Lorenzo, and a scattering of Gothic, Renaissance, and baroque palaces.
The church of San Zeno Maggiore, a fine Romanesque edifice, stands on the other side of the Castelvecchio. Its crypt holds the remains of Verona's first bishop (after whom the church is named) a man famous for his cheerful disposition. The church has many attractions. These include a tall brick bell-tower; a monumental bronze doorway with 48 panels framed in marble bas-reliefs; a triple barrel-vault arch; a triptych on the high altar, *Virgin and Child with Angels and Saints* by Mantegna;

THE TWELFTH-CENTURY
ROMANESQUE CHURCH
OF SANTO STEFANO IS
ONE OF THE OLDEST IN
VERONA.

THE PIAZZA BRÀ LIES AT THE FOOT OF THE VERONA ARENAS. THE WIDE CAFÉ-LINED SIDEWALK KNOWN AS THE LISTÓN IS BEST FOR LEISURELY STROLLING AT APERITIF TIME OR IN THE EVENING.

THE FOUNTAIN ON THE PIAZZA DELLE ERBE.

THE VILLA SAREGO AT SANTA SOFIA PEDEMONTE IN VALPOLICELLA.

THE CASA LAMBERTI.

an elegant rood screen with marble statuary; superb baptismal founts, and a cloister combining Romanesque and Gothic styles.

Those with an interest in ecclesiastical tourism should also pay a visit to Santa Maria Antica, where the Scaligers installed fine Gothic mausoleums; to Sant' Anastasia for the Antonio Pisanello fresco and two holy-water basins supported by stooping male figures; to the Duomo for its two Romanesque doorways and a Titian *Assumption*; to San Fermo Maggiore's two-churches-in-one (tombs and frescos); to San Bernardino for the Pellegrini chapel; to San Giorgio in Braida for two frescos by Tintoretto and Veronese; to Santo Stefano for the Chapel of the Innocents, and to Santa Maria in Organo for the very fine marquetry choir stalls.

Verona is notable more for its squares than for its streets. The spacious Piazza Brà is the place to take part in the daily Italian custom of *la passegiata*. As evening falls, people stroll idly along the Listón, a wide sidewalk of pink stone, stopping to greet friends and chat. The square attracts even larger crowds on nights when there is a performance in the adjacent Arena—a Roman amphitheater with a diameter of over 1,300 feet in which gladiators were once pitted against lions. For a Verdi or Puccini opera, the amphitheater can seat as many as 25,000 people. An open-air theater, of similar age, and built in the traditional semi-circular form, is used for more modest productions. It rises above the Adige on

THE VERONA ARENA
(*L'ARENA*) WAS
DAMAGED BY AN
EARTHQUAKE IN 1117,
BUT TODAY IT STILL
WELCOMES THRONGS OF
MUSIC LOVERS WHO
COME HERE EVERY YEAR
TO PAY TRIBUTE TO THE
LYRIC ARTS.

the opposite bank. On the Piazza dei Signori, closer to the center of the old town, stands a statue of Dante. The poet appears lost in thought. Perhaps he is wondering how to step down from his pedestal and enjoy a drink at the café bearing his name, the most elegant in Verona. Or perhaps he, too, is puzzling out the meaning of the Arco della Costa monument and its whalebone pendant— the presence of which no one can account for exactly. Is he contemplating the Renaissance era (represented by the lovely Loggia del Consiglio on the same square) that came after him? Does he dream of climbing the Torre dei Lamberti for a view of the Alps? Or is he regretting the fact he was not placed on another, neighboring square, less grandiose but more charming, the Piazza delle Erbe? This is where the city's main market is held. Here, the produce of this fertile region is displayed around an ancient fountain and at the feet of a Venetian lion. Framing the square are Gothic houses, former wheat granaries and the baroque Palazzo Maffei (now a hotel with an excellent restaurant).

The Verona countryside begins in the Veronetta section with the Giardino Giusti, an exquisite Renaissance park on two levels, one laid out geometrically, the other informally. Goethe liked to stroll

THE VILLA ALLEGRI-AVERDI IN GREZZANA. A SEVENTEENTH-CENTURY BAROQUE MANOR AT THE FOOT OF THE PICCOLE DOLOMITI RANGE.

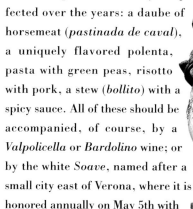

ENTRANCE TO THE MAFFEIANO MUSEUM IN VERONA.

here, and it is a favorite picnic spot for the local population.

Regretfully, we must now leave Verona behind and explore some of Venezia's other riches. But it would be a shame not to take the time to sample a few of the gastronomic specialties the city has perfected over the years: a daube of horsemeat (*pastinada de caval*), a uniquely flavored polenta, pasta with green peas, risotto with pork, a stew (*bollito*) with a spicy sauce. All of these should be accompanied, of course, by a *Valpolicella* or *Bardolino* wine; or by the white *Soave*, named after a small city east of Verona, where it is honored annually on May 5th with

SCULPTURE AT THE VILLA LA DELIZIOSA.

THE VALPOLICELLA
VINEYARDS ON THE
SLOPES ABOVE THE
RIVER OF THE SAME
NAME.

THE VALPOLICELLA
VINEYARDS ON THE
SLOPES ABOVE THE
RIVER OF THE SAME
NAME.

WINE CASK WITH
DECORATION PAINTED
BY CORTE SANT' ALDA.

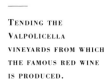

TENDING THE
VALPOLICELLA
VINEYARDS FROM WHICH
THE FAMOUS RED WINE
IS PRODUCED.

festivals evoking the many splendors of the Middle Ages. The Scaligers once owned a castle in this fortified city on the road to Vicenza. At nearby Montecchio Maggiore are the two romantic castles said to have belonged to the rival Montague and Capulet clans whose offspring, Romeo and Juliet, embarked on a fatal, forbidden love affair. From Soave we continue up the Alpone valley to Giazza, the center of a region known as "The Thirteen Towns." Recalling the "Seven Towns" region of Treviso, it too is marked by the same Bavarian tradition, as is amply illustrated in its ethnological museum. The mountain rises steeply above the Adige valley to the first peaks of the Dolomites, and there are a few ski resorts not too far from Verona. This is *Valpolicella* country, on the slopes surrounding the villages of Pedemonte, San Floriano, and San Pietro in Cariana. The road goes on, crossing the river and heading due north, after a hairpin bend, all the way to the *Bardolino* vineyards and Lake Garda. Venezia lies to the east of the lake, Lombardy to the west. The northern bank, narrowing between the mountains, is in Trentino-Upper Adige. But the olive groves around Lake Garda belong to Veneto, a city that once reigned supreme over the lake and still has a few palaces to show for it. Today it is a charming resort, and its café terraces fill with tourists in the summer. A small road leads to the San Vigilio promontory, a romantic

BERTANI

A LABEL COVETED BY
ALL LOVERS OF GOOD
WINE.

THE PLEASURES
OFFERED BY THE LAKE
ATTRACT NUMEROUS
VISITORS (ABOVE).

little port with its reeds and cypresses, its church, and the Villa Guarienti—a harbinger of the Renaissance. From there the road rises northward to Malcesine, at the foot of Monte Baldo (bald mountain), where Goethe was imprisoned in 1788 after being accused (falsely) of espionage. Or, one can take the road down to Bardolino, not just the name of a famous wine but also that of a charming resort in its own right; and to Lasize, originally a Veronese fortress and subsequently a port serving the Venetian Republic. These are all suitable bases from which to explore the lake itself or the countryside around it (a circuit of just under one hundred miles along a road that has some very beautiful stretches).

It would be a mistake not to venture out of Venezia into Lombardy, at least as far as Sirmione, whose fortress stands on a peninsula protruding into the lake from its south bank. It was built by the Scaligers (those powerful Veronese lords), who opposed the Viscontis here. By a quirk of administrative irony, the authorities have since placed Sirmione in Lombardy, but the ancient feuds and rivalries have now died down, and no journey to Venezia would be complete without a visit to this historic spot. From Sirmione's impressive Roman ruins, visitors can enjoy a splendid view over this lake that borders Venezia on the west, as the Adriatic Sea does on the east.

LAKE GARDA IS A
RAVISHING LITTLE
INLAND SEA BETWEEN
VENEZIA AND
LOMBARDY.

THE SIX MAIN STEPS TO
MAKING GNOCCHI.

PERCH WITH SAGE

Serves 6

12 fillets of perch, 2 eggs, pinch of salt, 1 cup breadcrumbs, ½ cup flour, 3 tbsps. olive oil, 4 tbsps. butter, 12 sage leaves, 1 lemon
For the Marinade:
2 cloves garlic, 1 onion, ¼ cup olive oil, 2 tbsps. white wine vinegar, 2 tbsps. dry white wine, salt, 3–4 black peppercorns, 12 leaves sage

Rinse the fillets of perch and drain on absorbent paper. Place all the ingredients for the marinade in a shallow bowl and mix. Add the fillets of perch. Allow to marinate for about 1 hour, turning from time to time. Remove the fillets from the marinade and wipe dry with a clean cloth. Beat the eggs in a bowl with a pinch of salt. Sift the breadcrumbs onto one plate, and the flour onto a second one. Dredge the fillets in the flour, dip in the beaten egg, and then dredge in the breadcrumbs. Heat the olive oil and half of the butter in a large skillet over a medium heat. When the oil and butter are sizzling hot, add the dredged fillets and cook until they are golden on both sides. Transfer the fillets to a warm serving dish. Add the remainder of the butter to the pan juices, and fry the sage leaves. Scatter the fried sage leaves over the fillets of perch, garnish with lemon wedges and serve.

GNOCCHI WITH DUCK STEW

Serves 6
The Gnocchi:
2 lbs. starchy potatoes (Idaho), 1 cup sifted flour, 1 egg, 1 tsp. grated nutmeg, salt

There is a knack to making gnocchi: patience! Preheat oven to 425°F. Wash the potatoes and boil, unpeeled, in 8 cups salted water. When they are cooked but still firm, remove from water and dry out in a hot oven for about 10 minutes. Peel them and put them through a ricer or vegetable mill placed over a bowl. Make a well in the center of the riced potatoes, beat the egg, and add. Add the sifted flour and grated nutmeg, mix well. Season with salt. Dip the hands in flour and then knead the potato mixture until smooth and thoroughly blended. If the dough sticks to the hands, add more flour. Form the gnocchi dough into a tubular shape and cut into pieces of about 1 inch each. Bring a large pot of water to a rolling boil, reduce the heat to a simmer. Add the gnocchi, which will sink to the bottom of the pot. When the gnocchi rise to the surface (after about 3 minutes) they are done. Use a skimmer to remove from the pot, and drain on absorbent paper. Gnocchi can be kept in the refrigerator, on a floured board, for up to one day.

The Duck Stew (Anitra in Salmi):
1 duck (with giblets) weighing 6 lbs., 3 cloves garlic, 2–3 sprigs rosemary, salt, pepper, tomato sauce (see recipe p. 92), 1 bunch parsley

Cut the duck into 6–8 pieces and arrange skin-side down in a heavy casserole. Do not add any fat or shortening. Add the garlic and rosemary. Cover and braise over low heat for 2 hours. Season with salt and pepper. Chop the giblets and add to the tomato sauce. Simmer for about 10 minutes. Chop the parsley and add to the tomato sauce mixture. Mix the sauce with the braised duck, or serve separately. If the duck is to be served with gnocchi, remove the bones, mix with the tomato sauce, and pour over the cooked gnocchi. Serve hot.

A POPULAR REFRAIN HEARD IN VERONA AT CARNIVAL-TIME IS, "RIDI, RIDI, CHE LA MAMMA HA FATTO I GNOCCHI" (LAUGH, LAUGH, MAMMA'S MADE GNOCCHI).

HARE WITH AMARONE

Serves 8

1 hare, 5 tbsps. butter, ¼ cup olive oil, 1 medium-thick slice strip bacon, flour, salt, 1 bottle Amarone or Secco Bertani de Valpolicella, 3 onions, 2 stalks celery, 2 carrots, 1 sprig rosemary, 1 sprig thyme, sage leaves, peppercorns, 6 cloves, 12 juniper berries, 1 bay leaf 1 cup chicken broth

Hare was traditionally marinated for several days to remove the gamy taste. But if the hare (or other game) is fresh, there will be no unpleasant taste, and the marinating time can be shorter.

Chop the onions, celery, and carrots. For the marinade, place the vegetables in a large bowl with the wine, herbs, and spices. Remove the giblets from the hare and set aside. Cut the hare into pieces and add to the marinade. Allow to marinate overnight. Take the pieces of hare out of the marinade, wipe dry, and dredge lightly in flour. Cut the rind off the bacon and discard. Chop the bacon and place in a heavy casserole with 3 tbsps. of the butter and a little olive oil. Add the pieces of hare and brown on all sides over medium heat. Add the marinade little by little, bring to a boil, reduce to a simmer, and cook over a low heat for 3 hours. Meanwhile, chop the giblets and simmer in the broth until they are cooked. When the pieces of hare are tender, remove them from the casserole and set them aside. Strain the cooking liquid into a bowl, then return it to the casserole. Add the pieces of hare and the giblets. Simmer briefly. Serve hot with freshly made yellow polenta and a bottle of the same wine used for making the sauce. This recipe is also suitable for other types of game.

VERONESE POT-AU-FEU

Serves 8

1 duckling, 1 Cotechino (Zampone-style) sausage, 2 lbs. beef (chuck, shoulder), 1 veal knuckle, 1 ox tongue, (*optional*: 8 marrow bones), 1 onion, 1 clove, 1 bouquet garni (bay leaves + parsley sprigs), 2 lbs. carrots, 1 lb. turnips, 1 small green cabbage, 3 leeks, 3 stalks celery

To preserve the flavor of the meat, it should be cooked in unsalted water, and the scum that rises to the surface during cooking should be removed with a skimmer at frequent intervals. Stud the onion with the clove. Fill a large pot with cold water. Add the beef, ox tongue, onion, and bouquet garni. Bring to a boil, reduce to simmer, and cook for about 1 hour, skimming frequently. Add the duckling and veal knuckle. Simmer 2 hours longer, skimming frequently. Meanwhile, place the sausage in a separate pot, cover with cold water, bring to the boil, reduce to simmer and poach for about 1 hour.

Wash and pare the rest of the vegetables, and add to the meat. Add the poached sausage, and continue cooking for about 30 minutes. Parboil the cabbage, and add to the rest of the ingredients. Simmer for a further 10 minutes.

When done, slice the meats and arrange on a serving platter with the vegetables. Moisten with a little broth. Serve with Cremona mustard (a fruit mustard made at Christmas-time with quince compote, mustard seeds, and caramelized candied fruit).

ZALETI BISCUITS

Serves 6

2 cups yellow cornmeal, 1½ cups flour, 3 eggs, ¾ cup sugar, ¾ cup butter, ¼ cup Corinth raisins, 4 tbsps. pine nuts, 3 oz. yeast, ½ cup milk, peel of 1 lemon, pinch of salt, 1 tsp. vanilla, confectioners' sugar

The literal translation of "zaleti" is "little yellow balls," referring to the color of the cornmeal from which they are made. These tiny rolls are traditionally eaten at carnival time, and are supposed to bring good luck.

Preheat oven to 350°F. Sift the cornmeal with the flour. Heat the milk to lukewarm. Dissolve the yeast in the milk. Soak the raisins in warm water to soften, drain, and set aside. Grate the lemon peel. Melt the butter. In a large bowl, beat the eggs with the sugar. Add the cornmeal and flour, salt, milk and dissolved yeast, raisins, pine nuts, grated lemon peel, melted butter, and vanilla. Stir with a wooden spoon until blended, adding a little milk if the dough is too stiff. Form tubes about 1–2 inches in diameter with the dough, and cut into pieces about 3 inches long. Place the rolls on a greased cookie sheet, allowing plenty of space between them. Bake for 25 to 30 minutes. When the zaleti are cooked, cool to lukewarm, and sprinkle with confectioners' sugar. Serve warm or cold.

CHERRIES WITH AMARONE

Serves 6

2 lbs. firm cherries (the Durone Marosticane variety found in Venezia is ideal), 1 cup Amarone, 3 tbsps. sugar, 2 cups vanilla ice-cream

Wash the cherries and remove the stems. Place the Amarone and sugar in a heavy pot, bring to a boil, reduce the heat, and simmer until the mixture reaches the syrup stage. Add the cherries, and poach in the syrup until soft. Remove from heat, cool, and serve over a scoop of ice-cream.

IN ITALY, THE BROTH FROM THIS RECIPE FOR VERONESE POT-AU-FEU IS NOT CUSTOMARILY SERVED AS A FIRST COURSE. IT IS SAVED FOR ANOTHER MEAL AND SERVED AS A SOUP, WITH THE SMALL TORTELLINI CALLED "VENUS'S NAVEL" OR FRESH PASTA ADDED. THE BROTH CAN ALSO BE USED FOR MAKING MEAT RISOTTO, PIGEON SOUP (SEE RECIPE P. 108), OR HARE WITH AMARONE (SEE RECIPE ON THIS PAGE).

PRACTICAL INFORMATION

————— ◄○► —————

ACCOMMODATION

VENICE
Palazzetto Pisani
San Marco, 2814
Tel.: (041) 528 5343

La Fenice
Campiello Fenice
San Marco, 1936
Tel.: (041) 523 2333

PADUA
Bellevue
Via L. Belludi, 11
Tel.: (049) 875 5547

TREVISO
Beccherie
Piazza Ancillotto, 10
Tel.: (042) 254 0871

LAKE GARDA
Biseti
Corso Italia, 34
Tel. (045) 725 5766

VERONA
Guilietta e Romeo
Vicolo Tre Marchetti, 3
Tel.: (045) 80 035

RESTAURANTS

VENICE
Antica Bessetta
Calle Savio
San Polo, 1395
Tel.: (041) 72 1687

Linea d'Ombra
Zattere ai Saloni
Dorsoduro, 19
Tel.: (041) 520 4720

PADUA
Osteria dalla Pasina
Via Peschiere, 15
Dosson di Casier
Tel.: (042) 238 2112

VERONA
Arche
Via Arche Scaligere, 6
Tel.: (045) 800 7415

THE DOLOMITES
Dolada
Via Dolada, 21
32010 Pieve d'Alpago
Tel.: (043) 747 9141

BIBLIOGRAPHY

Churches of Venice
Alessandra Boccato
Venice: Arsenale, 1999

*The Food of Venice: Authentic
Recipes from the City of Romance*
Luigi Veronelli
Boston: Periplus, 2001

Living in Venice
Frédéric Vitoux
Paris: Flammarion, 2000

The Stones of Venice
John Ruskin
New York: Da Capo Press, 1985

Venetian Life
William Dean Howells
Evanston: Northwestern University
Press, 2001

Venice
Alexandra Bonfante-Warren
New York: Friedman and Fairfax,
2000

RECIPE INDEX

—◄○►—